MILITANCY
and
ISLAM

BY THE SAME AUTHOR

War on Terror

MILITANCY
and
ISLAM

Edited by

Maj. Gen. (Retd.) Afsir Karim

The Forum for Strategic and Security Studies (FSSS), New Delhi

HAR-ANAND
PUBLICATIONS PVT LTD

HAR-ANAND PUBLICATIONS PVT LTD
E-49/3, Okhla Industrial Area, Phase-II, New Delhi-110020
Tel.: 41603490 Fax: 011-41708607
E-mail: haranand@rediffmail.com
Website: www.haranandpublications.com

Published by Ashok Gosain and Ashish Gosain for
Har-Anand Publications Pvt Ltd

Printed in India at Ram Book Banding House

Editor's Introduction

Islamic fundamentalism that translates into militancy is a phenomenon that must be analysed in depth to be understood with clarity. A characteristic common to all forms of fundamentalist-extremist ideologies is that they reject any other worldview except their own and invariably use violent means to impose their views.

Fundamentalist militants believe that acts of terrorism, against high-value targets and the power symbols of a targeted adversary are justified for creating a society based on their brand if Islam. Targeting of innocent civilians and terrorising an entire population is considered justified, terrorists believe that there are no innocent bystanders in this kind of war and a common man is a legitimate target. Fundamentalist terrorism, however, generally fail to achieve its long-term objectives because of strong aversion their brutal actions evoke among the people. The course of recent fundamentalist militant movements in various parts of the world suggests that such movements invariably degenerate into stark terrorism and continue regardless of failures. The most persistent form of fundamentalist militancy has been spawned by distorted application of Islamic values by certain extremist groups.

All forms of extremist violence cannot, however, be categorized as Islamic militancy, many violent movements with similar characteristics are not Islamic in character. Recent examples are terrorist cadres of the LTTE, the terrorists of Ireland, and many separatist groups in India and other countries.

The primary aim of Islamic militants in Asia has generally been to destabilise and overthrow targeted regimes by isolating them morally and physically from their domestic support bases and degrading their material resources and security infrastructure. Militant

Islam has assumed a menacing form in the recent years in different parts of South Asia and its threats are gradually becoming more virulent because it employs terrorism combined with armed insurgency and subversion as a means of undermining the secular and democratic traditions of targeted countries in a systematic manner. Militancy in such a scenario may take the shape of a protracted low intensity war waged with the aim of disrupting socio-economic cohesion and fomenting unrest and strife in targeted areas.

Ethnic, racial and religious tensions are considered essential for mobilisation of radical elements to fuel violence and conflicts, which are triggered through persistent terrorist strikes. Repeated terrorist strikes on sensitive targets like portals of democracy, places of worship escalate internal conflicts, create chaos and panic. The aim of major militant strikes may be summarised as under:

- Spreading violence in chosen areas to bring crucial commercial and administrative activities to a stand still
- Disrupting trade, industry and civic facilities
- Engineering provocative incidents to intensify ethnic and religious strife
- Carrying out catastrophic terrorist attacks to inflict mass casualties among common people
- Carrying out cyber or electronic pulse attacks to paralyse communication, command and communication networks

In Pakistan, the resurgent Jihadi forces have gained greater support, and al-Qaeda and the Taliban have more political acceptability than ever before, they now operate with impunity in various parts of Pakistan. In view of these developments, there is a need to assess whether Pakistan will gradually drift into fundamentalism and more people will join hands with the Taliban to fight the secular forces.

It appears that the future developments will lead to greater Jihadi violence and they may attain formidable strength if weapons of mass destruction are made available to them by a rouge sponsoring group or state. The rise of radical elements in India, Pakistan and Bangladesh and the acts of terror committed by them recently foretell escalation of violence in the entire South Asian region.

The terrorist threats are gradually becoming more lethal, and terrorism combined with armed insurgency and subversion has become a means of undermining the secular and democratic traditions of the targeted entities in an organized manner in several parts of the globe. Terrorism has already taken the shape of a protracted civil war waged with the aim of disrupting socio-economic cohesion, fomenting unrest and strife in several parts of Africa and Asia.

Al-Qaedism has appeared as a violence oriented ideology, and it has now spread to large parts of the globe. The physical assets of al-Qaeda are no longer centralised and the people inspired by its ideas cannot be targeted by security forces. Many experts believe that the biggest threat from al-Qaeda is not its strike capability but its ideas and the manner in which they inspire the disaffected and angry in Muslim communities worldwide. Invariably extremist ideologies of this kind and militancy lead to blocking the prospects of peace and contribute to the perpetuation of conflicts.

It has been rightly said 'Fundamentalists are advocates of a minority viewpoint. They see themselves as a righteous remnant. Even when they are numerically a majority, they perceive themselves as a minority. They are oppositional and confrontational towards both secularists and "wayward" religious followers. They are secondary level male elites led invariably by charismatic males. Fundamentalists generate their own technical vocabulary. Fundamentalism has historical antecedents, but no ideological precursor.'

The negative consequences of militancy and terrorism are, however, apparent every where, violence committed by extremists traumatize not only their opponents, but also their supporters and allies. Religious militancy though generally committed by a small minority is often attributed to the entire community which greatly harms its larger interests; it also creates disaffection and alienation leading to escalation of violence in peaceful societies.

Activities of Islamic militant groups trained and supported by al-Qaeda and others fundamentalist organizations have been regularly examined in-depth in regional and global context in several issues of *Aakrosh*. The Journal keeps a special watch on countries and non-state actors who encourage growth of fundamentalism, terrorism and internal conflicts with a view to destabilize secular regimes. Various facets of Islamic militancy that fuel regional conflicts have been analysed in *Aakrosh* through well-researched and scholarly case studies from time to time. A selection of ten essays that have been published in *Aakrosh* on the subject are being published in this volume.

Contents

CHAPTER 1

Al-Qaeda: The Base Expands

Pinaki Bhattacharya

On 5 February 2003, the then US Secretary of State, Gen Colin Powell had said at the United Nations Security Council (UNSC) that, "Iraq today harbors a deadly terrorist network, headed by Abu Musab al-Zarqawi, an associate and collaborator of Osama bin Laden and his al-Qaeda lieutenants." This was an important part of Powell's false case for an aggression against Iraq and its then president, Saddam Hussain. The world came to know of Zarqawi then for the first time. On 27 December 2004, Osama bin Laden, the emir of al-Qaeda, declared Zarqawi as the emir al-Qaeda (The Base) in Iraq. Powell's seemingly prophetic words bore fruit not when Saddam Hussain was at the helm, but when Iraq was under the occupation of the Anglo-American coalition. The Base found a new mentor. And the baton of the world's most dreaded Islamic terrorist passed on from Laden to Zarqawi.

With that ended the first phase of al-Qaeda's evolution. In this phase, Laden had sought to initiate the war against the 'faraway enemy'—the West, command the attention of the Islamic ummah, and spawn more Islamic warriors of his ilk. Holed up in the tribal territory of Pakistan-Afghanistan border with the world's biggest powers snapping at his heels, Laden's operational reach and effectiveness is clearly stretched and limited. In the past one year, the two spectacular terrorist actions had at best tenuous linkages to the al-Qaeda of the old guards. London's 7/7 and Jordan's November blasts were the handiwork of people who had borrowed at best, inspiration from Laden's al-Qaeda. The acts were clearly rooted in the region. Iraq is the new training ground for fundamentalist Islam's armed activists. Within three years of the ouster of the Taliban from Afghanistan, they have found another fertile ground.

Ayman al-Zawahiri, Laden's Egyptian deputy, wrote to their primary progeny Abu Musab al-Zarqawi, "I want to be the first to congratulate you for what God has blessed you with in terms of fighting battle in the heart of the Islamic world, which was formerly the field for major battles in Islam's history, and what is now the place for the greatest battle of Islam in this era, and what will happen, according to what appeared in the Hadiths of the Messenger of God about the epic battles between Islam and atheism. It has always been my belief that the victory of Islam will never take place until a Muslim state is established in the manner of the Prophet in the heart of the Islamic world, specifically in the Levant, Egypt, and the neighboring states of the Peninsula and Iraq; however, the center would be in the Levant and Egypt."[1] Clearly, the former had recognised the importance of the Iraq battlefield of Zarqawi. The purported letter was released to the global media by the US intelligence services in October.

The Jordan-born warlord in Iraq is doing the same as what Abdullah Azzam of Maktab *al-Khadamat* or Services (Arab-Afghan) Bureau and, later, Laden did in taking on the Soviet forces - seek to mutate their *jihad* into a pan-Islamic phenomenon. Experts notice trends in the Iraq battles that point at a propensity once seen with the Afghan Arabs (as Arabs who fought the Red Army in Afghanistan are known) as they returned to their home bases after ousting a superpower. These Afghanistan returnees had begun the process of radicalising their communities against their own regimes or the 'near enemy' in West Asia—those that were firmly aligned with the USA. Laden's mid-1998 *fatwa* declaring the war against the USA, "the

[1]"English translation of Ayman al-Zawahiri's letter to Abu Musab al-Zarqawi," *The Weekly Standard*, Washington, 12 October 2005, <http://www.weeklystandard.com/Content/Public/Articles/000/000/006/203gpuul.asp?pg=1>.

occupier of the land of the two Holy places" had overridden his foot soldiers' own little wars.

This time around, with the Iraq 'war' on, al-Qaeda has planned a different strategy. After Afghanistan and after the Saudi Arabian regime refused Laden's help to oust Saddam Hussain's forces from Kuwait, the former realised the pre-eminence of the USA in his territory. It came to him in starker reality in Sudan, especially after his eventual ouster from Khartoum. Returning to Kabul, his old stomping ground, under the influence of his new post-Azzam ideological guide, al-Zawahiri, Laden set his sights on the USA. Be that as it may, the son of the Saudi civil contractor was still hamstrung tactically because of the lack of a strategic location.

Mullah Omar's band of Afghan zealots might have granted a free run of their land for setting up training and indoctrination camps. But, Afghanistan was too inconveniently located geographically to be a staging post to oust the USA and the Jews from West Asia/ Middle East and establish a 'caliphate'. Post-9/11, George W. Bush's America has given Laden the precise opportunity he was in search of; Iraq in the heart of the Arabian peninsula. Reality of this kind, the neo-conservative dogmatists in Washington may have not factored in their simplistic theological vision of the world and the USA's role.

Ayman al-Zawahiri does not suffer from any such illusions of grandeur. Clearly, he knows the challenges ahead. So, in his letter to Zarqawi, he has clearly enunciated the tactical goals ahead. By that action, he has also acknowledge Zawqawi's position as the next torch-bearer of al-Qaeda. In his letter, he wrote, "The second stage, establish an Islamic authority or emirate, then develop it and support it until it achieves the level of a caliphate over as much territory as you can to spread its power in Iraq, i.e., in Sunni areas, is in order to fill the void stemming from the departure of the Americans, immediately upon their exit and before un-Islamic forces attempt to fill this void, whether those whom the Americans will leave behind them, or those among the un-Islamic forces who will try to jump at taking power.

There is no doubt that this emirate will enter into a fierce struggle with the foreign infidel forces, and those supporting them among the local forces, to put it in a state of constant preoccupation with defending itself, to make it impossible for it to establish a stable state which could proclaim a caliphate, and to keep the Jihadist groups in a constant state of war, until these forces find a chance to annihilate them.

The third stage, extend the *jihad* wave to the secular countries neighbouring Iraq."[2] The goal is to hunker down for a protracted war. George W. Bush will not be a president after 2008, and even the Republican Party may not be leading the US policies. But Zarqawi or someone like him, baked in the crucible of Iraq, will be around. Unlike Laden who shares the Saudi elites' inclination for working their way around problems by writing cheques, Zarqawi knows the meaning of hunkering down. Born in an underprivileged family, Zarqawi's restless youth saw him in jail for the first time on charges of drug possession and sexual assault.[3]

His story then takes the usual contours of the account of most Arab terrorists. Getting indoctrinated in jail, he was recruited for Afghanistan in 1989. But, arriving in Kabul, he discovered that the war was over. Even as he began working at the Arab-Afghan Bureau as a minor factotum, he befriended a Palestinian named Abu Muhammad al-Maqadisi. Maqadisi has been described as a radical Islamic thinker of the Salafi[4] School of Islamic jurisprudence, closely aligned with Wahhabism in its literalist interpretation of the early Islamic texts like the Q'uran.

Soon the two returned to Jordan where they began their radical enunciations. They were both jailed—a second time for Zarqawi—for 15 years. Again, the jail term toughened Zarqawi more. He grew

[2]Call it what you may, insurgency or a battlefield in the war 'War Against Terrorism,' Iraq is still in war.

[3]Loretta Napoleoni, "Profile of a Killer," *Foreign Policy*, November-December 2005, <http://www.foreignpolicy.com/story/cms.php?story_id=3264>.

[4]*Ibid.*

stronger physically and mentally. Becoming a leader among the inmates, his devotion to Islam increased. Released in an amnesty in 1999, after seven years behind bars, he set out to reach Chechnya through Pakistan,[5] and possibly the Central Asian route. Pakistan authorities pushed him into Afghanistan under the Taliban after a proforma arrest for an expired visa.[6]

On this trip, he met Osama bin Laden, with whom he differed on the conception of their *jihad.* For Zarqawi, the 'near enemy'—the corrupt, degenerate and alienated regimes of West Asia, tied in their entrails to the USA—were a more immediate target, than the 'faraway enemy' of Laden's.[7] After the Taliban's ouster in 2002, Zarqawi moved to northern Iraq's Kurdistan. He in a nationalist fervour, largely led by the Iraqi Shi'ite leader Muqtada al-Sadr waited patiently even as Iraq erupted after Saddam Hussain's fall and the Anglo-American occupation.

Zarqawi woke up to action when Sadr began to take on the image of a hero in the eyes of the Iraqi Sunnis. Prevailing Western notions believe that Zarqawi was stirred to action when he realized that an Iraqi Shi'ite-Sunni nationalist coalition will cut the ground from under the feet of an al-Qaeda-like organisation.[8] This would have denied them the best opportunity yet to translate their vision of Islam in a region that is the heartland, West Asia. He sought the stamp of authority from Laden, which the latter provided to him in an audio address in December 2004 - the last time Laden was heard of. Apparently, Zarqawi was not Laden's first choice to lead his brand of *jihad* in Iraq. Their backgrounds were too disparate. And, Laden may have remembered Zarqawi's Bedouin petulance in publicly disagreeing with him earlier.

[5] *Ibid.*
[6] *Ibid.*
[7] *Ibid.*
[8] *Ibid.*

Ayman al-Zawahiri's letter shows how acutely aware of the Muslim public opinion the al-Qaeda leadership is in this current phase of their war. At one place he wrote, ".... If we look at the two short-term goals, which are removing the Americans and establishing an Islamic amirate in Iraq, or a caliphate if possible, then, we will see that the strongest weapon which the mujahedeen enjoy—after the help and granting of success by God—is popular support from the Muslim masses in Iraq, and the surrounding Muslim countries.

So, we must maintain this support as best we can, and we should strive to increase it, on the condition that striving for that support does not lead to any concession in the laws of the Sharia.

And it's very important that you allow me to elaborate a little here on this issue of popular support. Let's say:

If we are in agreement that the victory of Islam and the establishment of a caliphate in the manner of the Prophet will not be achieved except through *jihad* against the apostate rulers and their removal, then this goal will not be accomplished by the mujahed movement while it is cut off from public support, even if the Jihadist movement pursues the method of sudden overthrow. This is because such an overthrow would not take place without some minimum of popular support and some condition of public discontent, which offers the mujahid movement what it needs in terms of capabilities in the quickest fashion. Additionally, if the Jihadist movement were obliged to pursue other methods, such as a popular war of jihad or a popular intifadah, then popular support would be a decisive factor between victory and defeat...."[9]

Clearly, the goal is to win a public relations war in Iraq and then fan outwards. Laden's *jihad* has finally reached the region, which he intended all along the way. The nation on his cross hairs is the one with the two Holy places, Saudi Arabia. Therefore, Zawahiri is worried with Zarqawi's targeting philosophy. The latter seems to be killing more Muslims than Americans or their allies. His current

[9] *Ibid.*

Amman bombing blew up a marriage party of well-off Muslims leading to street protests in Jordan. As the fourth year of WOT (War on Terrorism) draws to a close, al-Qaeda is in the cusp of time.

Reportedly, the al-Saud family of a few thousand-odd princelings has written a few more cheques to buy peace with al-Qaeda, but that may only be temporary.[10] Evidence exists that Laden's organisation has deeply penetrated the Saudi police and armed forces.[11] With a few thousand Saudi nationals fighting against the US and allied forces in Iraq, their eventual return may well signal the beginning of the struggle to unseat the Saudi rulers. Historical parallels between Prophet Mohammad's battles to take control of the area from the pagans and al-Qaeda's quasi-religious quest abound.

But, this classic historical inversion has lessons for many potential rulers who find the potent mix of religion with politics a sure recipe for success. The founder of al-Saud family Muhammad ibn-Saud, who ruled a principality called Darriyah, had given refuge to Ibn Abd al-Wahhab - the founder of Wahhabism - fleeing an arrest by the Ottoman rulers as he had sought to challenge their Islamic credentials.[12] In 1747, al-Saud and Ibn Abd al-Wahhab evolved a power sharing formula by which the former became the political potentate, while the latter became the unquestioned religious authority. It suited both as they complemented each other's strengths.

Extending their territory with pillage, plunder and sacking of historical treasures, the al -Saud-al-Wahhab clan took control of much of the Arab peninsula.[13] In 1787, al-Wahhab declared himself the 'caliph' of the world-wide Islamic *ummah*. To back this travesty of reality, he also issued a *fatwa* (edict) calling for a *jihad* against the

[10]*Op cit*, n.1.

[11]Richard L. Russell, "Insurgency in Waiting," *Foreign Policy*, November 2005, <http://www.foreignpolicy.com/story/cms.php?story_id=3309>.

[12]*Ibid.*

[13]Stephen Schwartz, *The Two Faces of Islam*, New York: Anchor Books, A Division of Random House, Inc., September 2003.

Ottomans. The latter, Muslims themselves, were then taking on the British imperial forces seeking to gain control of Arabia. Abd al-Aziz Ibn Saud, who had succeeded Mohammad ibn-Saud after his death, joined hands with the same British to take control to Kuwait in 1889 after defeating the Ottomans.[14] This had laid the foundations of the Saudi rulers long association with the Christian West, in their quest to become the pre-eminent power controlling the two Holy sites of Islam—thus control the minds and bodies of millions of Muslims worldwide. British and later, the Americans were happy with this arrangement as they found the al-Saud family immensely pliable to their ministrations, thus in effect controlling the Islamic forces through them.

Laden has challenged this *status quo*. Moreover, he has tapped into a welter of resentment against the Saudi regime and other West Asian regimes of its ilk. Popular resentment at their opulent excesses and licentious lifestyles is at its peak.[15] Coupled with that is the realisation that a bulk of the oil proceeds these countries earn go into the bottomless pit of greed of these rulers or flow back to the Western corporations in the form of various revenue drawbacks. Ironically, Laden is seeking to harness this public anger by creating a vision of Islamic Puritanism of the same Wahhabi/Salafi school that had for so long propped up these regimes.

Prophet Mohammad might have had an inkling of what could befall his followers with the vigilantism of the likes of Ibn Abd al-Wahhab, Ibn Taymiyyah and the like. A *Hadith* recording shows the Prophet praying aloud and asking "O Allah, give us blessings in our Syria, O Allah, give us blessings in our Yemen." Someone called out asking him to add a prayer for Najd, a place adjacent to Mecca and Medina, now in Saudi Arabia. But the Prophet ignored him. The onlooker insisted again that a prayer for Najd be included. This time the Prophet turned around and replied, "From that place will come

[14] *Ibid.*
[15] *Ibid.*

only earthquakes, conflicts and the horns of Satan."[16] Ibn Abd al-Wahhab, the founder of the Wahhabism of the Saudi rulers, and Osama bin Laden were born in Najd.

More than such a prophecy, a clear and present danger lies in the sentiments expressed by al-Zawahiri in his letter to Zarqawi. He wrote, "...The battles that are going on in the far-flung regions of the Islamic world, such as Chechnya, Afghanistan, Kashmir, and Bosnia, they are just the groundwork and the vanguard for the major battles which have begun in the heart of the Islamic world. We ask God that He send down his victory upon us that he promised to his faithful worshipers."[17] The year 2006 may witness the expansion of such battles in West Asia.

Does that mean that al-Qaeda will stop taking the battles into the nations of the West they consider their primary targets as they did in Madrid and in London? The answer to that lies in the fact that these tactical actions will possibly now be more closely aligned to the central theatre of operations—West Asia. Al-Qaeda may use the London- or Madrid-like blasts to focus global attention on an issue that might emerge in the central theatre or attenuate a strategic requirement of the same area.

Curiously, a man who is holed up in an isolated corner of the world—the Afghanistan-Pakistan border—al-Zawahiri is acutely conscious of public opinion. He wrote to Zarqawi that half of this war is being fought in the media.[18] And half of that battle the West is losing. Reports of prisoner abuse in Guantanamo Bay, Abu Ghraib in Iraq or even pictures emerging from the streets of Baghdad show a certain attitudinal change amongst the Western leadership that does not augur well for the world order. They seem to have quietly acquiesced to the violation of national and international laws governing human rights in this WOT.

[16] *Ibid.*
[17] *Ibid.*
[18] Op cit n.1.

If the former chief of staff Col Lawrence Wilkerson is to be believed, "I don't think in our history we've ever had a Presidential involvement, a Secretarial involvement, a Vice-Presidential involvement, an Attorney General involvement in telling our troops that, essentially, carte blanche is the way you should feel. You should not have any qualms because this is a different kind of conflict ... I understand the radical change in the nature of our enemy, but that doesn't mean we make a radical change in the nature of America. But that's what we did. And we did it in private. And we did it in such privacy that the Secretary of State had to open the door to my office one day ... and he said, "Larry. Larry, get everything. Get all the paperwork. Get the ICRC (International Community of the Red Cross) reports. Get everything. I think this is going to be a real mess...."[19] He was speaking at the New America Foundation, Washington, in mid-October 2005.

Col Wilkerson is not squeamish about using deadly force. But as a soldier and an American, as he says, he is worried about the sharp fall that a regime he was a part of has led his country. A crucial part of the paragraph quoted above is his recognition of the "radical change in the nature of the enemy." Secretary of State, Condoleezza Rice, recently on a trip to Europe for controlling the fall-out from the public exposure of secret CIA flights and ultra-secret CIA prisons for Islamic terrorists in Europe, prefaced each of her statements justifying US action with the words that these were "terrorists" who pose a threat to common people. Unsaid in her statements was the sub-text, that in their treatment anything goes. In other words, the 'Geneva Convention relative to the Treatment of Prisoners of War' of 1949 that guided Allied treatment of Axis POWs of World War II has little meaning in official Washington.

[19]Col Lawrence Wilkerson, former chief of staff to the former US secretary of state, Gen Colin Powell, speaking at the New America Foundation, Washington, 19 October 2005, <http://www.newamerica.net/index.cfm?Pg=event&EvelD=520>.

Unfortunately for the 49 per cent of American voting public who did not elect George W. Bush in 2004, the 51 per cent who elected him obviously support these US government actions. But as a corollary of that, 100 per cent of the Americans and indeed the Britons face the heightened tyranny of Zarqawi's men. The latest batch of five Westerners led by Canadian aid workers - snatched in Iraq - were televised wearing orange jump suits that has entered the global political imagery as the uniform of the inmates of dreaded Guantanamo. Now, an organisation like al-Qaeda is not even a party to the Geneva Convention. Yet, for those who deal with the minefield of hostage negotiation, a large quotient is the captors' conscience. It is common among security forces around the world to see wisdom in humane treatment of captured enemy combatants as a concomitant of a similar treatment if the dice rolls the other way. Reports of ill treatment by the Western forces obviate even such nebulous *quid pro quos* in this increasingly 'dirty WOT'.

Each of the items in the increasing din of news reports of prisoner abuse is a public relations windfall for the al-Qaeda, in the same way the Vietnam War was for the Soviet Union in the Third World. Increasing sophistication of al-Qaeda operations points at their enhanced understanding of these facts. They may also signal a crucial change within the al-Qaeda with Laden turning into a figurehead with real control passing into the hands of the *jihadi* from Egypt, al-Zawahiri. The former has not been seen or heard of since December 2004 while the latter has addressed the world audience at least four times in 2005.

From the beginning, in contrast to Laden's rag-tag associates, al-Zawahiri led on intellectually capable group of doctors, engineers, and trained soldiers.[20] An ailing Laden is completely dependent on the Egyptian doctor for medical care. The sharp medic has also posted his trusted, key lieutenants in Laden's entourage over the

[20]Lawrence Wright, "The man behind Bin Laden: How an Egyptian doctor became a master of terror," *New Yorker*, New York, 16 September 2005, <http://www.newyorker.com/fact/content/articles/020916fa_fact2a>.

years.[21] Some would think that the temporary truce he had struck about the conception of the *jihad*, by which al-Zawahiri had acquiesced to Ladenite ideas of taking on the 'distant enemy', the USA at the expense of operations against Arab regimes[22] may not now be necessary. With Iraq as the focal point of al-Qaeda operations, he now can argue his tactical line that the West Asian regimes and the USA can both be attacked in one theatre. This will add more weight to the possible reasons that led to his missive to Zarqawi.

Curiously, this can also signal a modicum of tactical success for the Anglo-American coalition. After 9/11, the biggest problem the USA faced with al-Qaeda and bin Laden was that they were not wedded to any territory. Pinning them down thus became all the harder. Now if the al-Qaeda chooses to fight its war in West Asia/ Middle East, it can suit policy makers in Washington and London for it is far away from their home bases and is something they can deal with purely militarily. After that fateful September, it does appear that the threshold of the American public for absorbing armed forces loss of lives has increased enormously.

Of course, what it does to the public opinion in a region immensely important for its oil wealth for the energy guzzling Western economies is a different issue. But to understand this aspect one needs to take a quick look at the US oil strategy as was envisioned in the US's National Energy Policy Development Group, headed by the redoubtable vice president of the USA, Richard (Dick) B. Cheney. The USA consumes 25 per cent of all the oil produced in the world annually.

Almost 24 per cent of that consumption is accessed from the region the US calls the Middle East.[23] Though the country as a policy has been shifting its energy supplies away from the Arab

[21] *Ibid.*

[22] *Ibid.*

[23] *National Energy Policy*, May 2001, Report of the (US) National Energy Policy Development Group.

countries to the Western hemisphere since the first 'oil shock' of the 1970s, it still acknowledges that the former will be playing a key role in the global energy security with 67 per cent of the proven oil reserves till date.[24] In the new dispensation, the latest playground for the USA's - indeed the West's - quest for secure oil in Central Asia.

Ironically, Islam is a predominant force in that region also. Yet, for those who search for an Islam that is not at odds with modernism while being at peace with itself, Central Asia may hold the key. For in that region Islam had reached the Ottoman/Turkic way, rooted in cultural modernism. Potentially, here and currently in the Balkans where the Slavs converted to Islam, the Wahhabi/Salafi Islam of bin Laden-al-Zawahiri-Zarqawi brand will face the biggest intra-Islam challenge. Iran, along with Turkey, may prove to be the main instigator of the challenge to the Islamist *ummah* vision of the trio.

A classic example of this tussle is available in the words of Reis-ul-Ulema, Mustafa Ceric of Bosnia-Herzegovina who said in May 2005 when charged that the region was becoming a hotbed for Ladenite *jihadi* Islam in Europe, "... you need to ask what Wahhabism actually is. There is a political and a religious Wahhabism; the political form was created by the west of defeat the Ottoman Empire. Saudi Arabia is still the ally of the west. Ideological Wahhabism, the theology, is alien to us Bosnian Muslims. We have a different understanding of state and society. The Bosnian Muslims will not change in that respect, you can be sure of that."[25]

He even suggests a way for the Muslims in Europe to find a unified vision. Ceric prescribes, "I live for the day when Europe's Muslims will have the chance to be successful and make their

[24] *Ibid.*

[25] For an Indian reader suffused in Deobandi School of Islamic thought, deeply entangled with Wahhabism, Euro-Islam may be a new concept. For the interview with the Reis-ul-Ulema, read, <http://www.qantara.de/webcom/show_article.php/_c-478/_nr-105/i.html.>.

contribution toward a united Europe. I am not concerned about our future as a religious community in Bosnia, more so about the community in Western Europe. Here we have the Reis-ul-Ulema, the highest religious authority, while in Western Europe there are hundreds of Islamic groups with a wide range of different views.

We in Bosnia have a long, firmly established tradition. In Western and Central Europe there are immigrant societies whose members may have lived there for three or four generations but are still quite fragmented all the same. That is why I believe the Muslims in Europe must develop a unified representative agency. That would be in Europe's interest. Our religious teachers ought to be trained in Europe and regard themselves as European Muslims. That would also mean accepting the values of European society regarding freedom and the rule of law and continuing to develop them."[26]

Asked whether the 'Clash of Civilisations' has already begun as exemplified by the al-Qaeda, Ceric makes bold, "I completely reject this notion. The path we are on is a different one. We are experiencing the development from slavery to freedom, from the law of the jungle to a democratic state under the rule of law. The world can thank western civilization for this development, especially Europe. The legitimization of the state, that is, democracy, is one of the greatest achievements ever.

But now these values are no longer tied to western civilization, they are values that others accept and claim for themselves. What is happening now actually represents a crisis of western civilization, which obviously does not want to share these values with others."[27]

He argues that the continuous migration of Muslims from the East to the West signifies that the Muslims do not reject the chance to open up towards the West.[28] Clearly, his indication is towards a contrary vision of the 'retrenchment of modern society' portrayed by suicide bombers and the like.

[26] *Ibid.*
[27] *Ibid.*
[28] *Ibid.*

Islamic thinkers around the world are grappling with the internal crisis of the religion triggered by organisations like al-Qaeda. A Moroccan philosopher, Mohammad Sabila describes the current situation rather succinctly. An advocate for a self-critique of Islam, Sabila argues, "When I speak of self-critique, I mean that the Muslim cultural heritage must be subjected to historical and rational critique. It requires the outsider perspective, especially in the human and social sciences, a perspective based on human knowledge. Self-critique in the Islamic world refers to both internal and external critique. Islamic fundamentalists understand critique as aggression that is rooted in thinking borrowed from the West."[29]

Asked whether Islam needs a critique from the West, Sabila seeks an understanding based on a correct identification of the multi-faceted influences of the West. He argues, "Yes. Because what is described as the West is multi-layered. There are at least two components: the West as the *avant-garde* of humanity, the leading force in scientific accomplishment, and the West as a repressive colonial power. Thinkers like Foucault or Adorno and the Frankfurt School have criticised instrumental reason and its tendency towards external as well as internal exploitation.

When the extremists say to us the West embodies repression, we reply that they must distinguish between the ideology or the will to power and scientific progress. There was a movement towards cultural and political renaissance in the middle of the 19th century in the Arab world as well. The Egyptian revolution was the result of this opening to the rest of the world. After the occupation of Palestine and the aggression of some Western powers in 1956, public opinion shifted and the Arab world retreated into its own cultural heritage."[30]

[29]Mohammad Sabila serves as a consultant in the Ministry of Human Rights in Morocco. This interview with him throws up the internal contradictions among religious Muslims with the *Jihadi* philosophy. <http://www.qantara.de/webcom/show_article.php/_c-476/_nr-426/i.html>.

[30]*Ibid.*

Ironically, this characteristic separatism of Islamists cannot be found in the Prophet and he might not have approved of it. For, when he himself was ousted from Mecca and had to take shelter in Medina, where the city council had invited him, he did not burrow into his band of loyal followers to seek shelter from the rest of the world. He established a just and a tolerant regime in Medina as a shining example of Islam's influence, continued proselytising and eventually raised an army to return to Mecca. Each of these acts signals proaction.

Ferghana Valley of Central Asia is an important battleground for many of these conflicting ideas. Colonised by the Russians, Soviet communism had injected modernism through industrial development. But many of the five nations of the region wallow in abject poverty, while sitting on rich natural resources. After these nations gained independence in the early 1990s, the region witnessed a spurt in Islamism. This came in conflict with their political forces that had merely taken off their Soviet labels and had transmuted into nationalist forces. Hence, the authoritarian instincts of the rulers had not changed. As the latter sought to tackle the religious by the use of force, organisations like Hizb-el-Tehrir raised their head to channelise popular anger.

West Asian nations like Saudi Arabia jumped into the fray to stoke the flames of Wahhabism riding on their financial resources. Reports indicate that each member of organisations like Hizb-el-Tehrir is paid $20-50 a month in a region where typically a teacher or a doctor earns $2-7 per month.[31] Michael Lüders, a German political scientist recently wrote a book *Tee im Garten Timurs* (Tea in the Garden of Timur).[32] He has been quoted as talking about

[31]Tobias Asmuth (trans. Aingeal Flanagan), "Islamists in Tajikistan: Fragile Peace Teetering on the Brink," Qantara.de 2005, 21 January 2005, <http://www.qantara.de/webcom/show_article.php/_c-476/_nr-308/i.html>.

[32]Ute Schaeffer (trans. Aingeal Flanagan), "Michael Lüders: Islamism in Central Asia," Deutsche Welle/dw-world.de 2003, 21 October 2003, <http://www.qantara.de/webcom/show_article.php/_c-476/_nr-37/i.html>.

three kinds of Islam being practiced in the region, "traditional Islam; radical Islam—which is the result of the interaction of political repression, the search for an identity and economic collapse—and official, governmental Islam, which serves primarily to legitimate authoritarian regimes.

While poverty in Central Asia is a breeding ground for radical ideologies, 70 years of the Soviet Union and state-imposed atheism have advanced the secularisation of the societies there. This is why radical Islam seems so utterly out of place in the Central Asian republics. More so than anywhere else.

Traditional Islam in this region is much more of a popular religion: a mythical, mystical popular faith that is tolerant, meditative and peaceful. This is why the political instability of the region is less the result of an Islamic factor—as the regimes continually seek to emphasise, in the hope of attracting (bigger amounts of) money from the West—and more the result of a lack of legitimacy for the regimes and their powerlessness to stop economic collapse and social injustice."[33]

Many of the groups active in the region are reported to have ties with the Al-Qaeda. But, in most cases, these linkages are blown up many times more by the local regimes only to garner greater Western attention. But, can Wahhabism counter the strong Sufi influence on Central Asian Islam—what Lüders calls traditional Islam? Money pouring in from various West Asian nations, through so-called non-governmental organisations (NGOs) practicing religio-social activism, may prove to be the key determinant.

Most importantly, however, the ultimate fate of the Anglo American forces in the battlefields of West Asia will be the crucial factor to determine whether Euro-Islam of Central Asia's "traditional Islam" can hold their own.

In sum, in the months ahead the condition in the West Asian theatre may actually deteriorate with the al-Qaeda sharpening its

[33] *Ibid.*

attacks. Eventually, a victory in WOT will narrow down to whether the Anglo-American coalition can continue to commit vast resources, or whether the al-Qaeda is able to expand its silent support -base and its operational bridgehead in Iraq. Considering the asymmetry among the contending forces in the existing battles, the real test will be the protracted nature of the war and the ability of either party to withstand the tests of time. Significantly, no victory may prove to be decisive. For the warring parties have already taken positions, which indicate historical continuum.

In this template of events, a possible capture of bin Laden by the allies of WOT may well have lost its operational relevance even in the larger sense. For, by the mood of Muslims around the world, the US and the UK may have already lost the moral high around, which is an essential element in any conflict. Post-conflict, this lowest common multiple normally helps to heal the psychological scars. As it appears now, a viable exit strategy may not exist for either party in this environment of high attrition. A Cold War has been replaced by a Fungible War—a state of permanent turmoil.

CHAPTER 2

Is the Taliban Being Converted into a *Jihadi* Army?

Sreedhar

Pakistan's persistence with the Taliban for the last five years, and the Taliban's actions in its immediate and extended neighbourhood are raising a number of questions about the Pakistan-Taliban combine. One argument could be that Pakistan wants to extend its sphere of influence in this region militarily through the Taliban. Is the Taliban being converted into a jihadi *army or an Islamic army with Pakistan extending all support covertly?*

The manpower for this jihadi *army appears to be largely from the radical Islamic elements that fought against the Red Army in Afghanistan in the 1980s. According to one estimate, more than 100,000 radicals from over 40 countries underwent military training in training camps in Pakistan and Afghanistan.*

The necessary resources for sustaining such an army are coming from the narcotics trade and smuggling activities of various elements. During 1997-99, the opium production in Taliban-controlled Afghanistan showed sharp increases, reaching an all-time high of 4,600 metric tonnes in 1999. With the international prices of narcotics touching an all-time high in 1999 too, the Taliban seem to have collected over $100 million as tax. Similarly, the smuggling trade through Afghanistan, estimated to be around $50 million in the 1980s, is currently estimated to be around $5 billion, enabling the organisers of the jihadi *army in the Pakistan-Taliban combine to reap huge profits.*

This jihadi *army so far proved to be successful only in terrorism and violence in various parts of the neighbourhood. Whenever they confronted professional armies like those of Iran, India and Russia, they quickly retreated. Currently, this* jihadi *army phenomenon is localised to Pakistan-Afghanistan, and their survival is dependent on the narcotics trade and smuggling activities.*

THE PAKISTAN-TALIBAN EQUATION

To understand the future of the Taliban in the Afghan context and in South and South West Asian regional politics, four factors need to be taken into consideration. The foremost among them would be that landlocked Afghanistan's dependence on neighbouring Pakistan for its very existence increased gradually from 1980 onwards. This dependence took a quantum jump after the Taliban came on the scene in 1994 and captured Kabul in September 1996. Though adjoining Turkmenistan and Iran do provide transit trade routes, yet around 75-80 per cent of Afghan trade is through Pakistan. Some of the important commodities that go from Pakistan include petroleum products, food grains and other essential commodities.

This excessive dependence on Pakistan is primarily due to Islamabad's decisive role in the creation of the Taliban movement and in making it a success by extending military and material support at every stage since the Taliban's inception.

Similarly, most of the Taliban's exports, from narcotics to re-export of luxury goods obtained from Dubai via Teheran are brought first to Peshawar and then they get into other distribution channels.

This entire economic interaction between Pakistan and the Taliban's Afghanistan is legalised by the Afghanistan Trade and Transit Agreement of 1965 between the two countries.

Second, Pakistan's Afghanistan policy operates at two levels. At the ground level it is coordinated and conducted by the Inter-Services Intelligence (ISI) within the overall command and control of the Pakistani chief of army staff. In 1988, Gen. Zia-ul-Haq's sudden death in a plane crash and the return of civilian rule brought in a new element. The civilian government of Benazir Bhutto during its second term (1993-96) perceived that the army's Afghan policy resulted in strained relations with its immediate neighbours. Therefore, she started articulating a policy of distancing itself from the Taliban. However, with the armed forces being the final arbiters of power in Pakistan, this policy never got translated into action. In addition, the Pakistan Army looked upon the Taliban's success as a unique opportunity to neutralise the traditionally hostile western neighbourhood.[1] In fact, one Pakistani scholar told the author that the Pakistani armed forces since the time of Gen. Mirza Aslam Beg (1988-91) onwards think that they have succeeded whereas their predecessors, both civil and military, had failed for the preceding four decades.[2]

One can debate endlessly on whether the Taliban was created by Pakistan or is an indigenous phenomenon.[3] But the past five and a half years of the history of the Taliban clearly shows that they quickly eliminated or neutralised all the anti-Pakistan elements in the Afghan polity. Either by design or by circumstance, they dovetailed their economy with that of Pakistan. The presence of Pakistani personnel in the Taliban structure ensured that the Taliban never deviated from the course predetermined for it by Pakistan.

[1]See the chapter on Pakistan in Sreedhar and Mohinder Ved, 1999, *Afghan Turmoil, Changing Equations*. New Delhi: Himalaya.

[2]The meeting took place in New Delhi in the summer of 1999. The scholar wanted to remain anonymous.

[3]There are any number of versions about the origin of the Taliban movement. That it is an indigenous movement was argued by Ahmed Rashid: 2000, *Taliban: Islam, Oil and the New Great Game in Central Asia*, New York: I. B. Taurus Publishers. Also see William Maley (ed.), 1998, *Fundamentalism Reborn? Afghanistan and the Taliban*, Lahore: Vanguard Books. For 'Taliban is a Creation of Pakistan', see Sreedhar and Mohinder Ved, 2000, *Afghan Buzkashi, Power Games and Gamesmen*, New Delhi: Wordsmith. Also Musa Khan Jalalzai, 1999, *Taliban: The Great Game in Afghanistan*, Lahore: Vanguard.

Third, the presence of the Taliban provided some advantages to Pakistan. At one level, the Pakistani government never got itself overtly involved in the Taliban's activities. However, the Taliban is flooded with volunteers from Pakistani madrassas and political parties like the Jamiat-ul-Ulema-e-Islam of Pakistan. Simultaneously, Pakistani officials from the armed forces and the ministries were posted right down to grass-roots levels to control the Taliban's administration. The official explanation given by Islamabad for this action is that they are not in a position to control the movement of people as the border between the two countries is an open one. This, more or less, blurred the Durand Line (the boundary between Pakistan and Afghanistan), which is what the former wants.

At another level, the way the Taliban was allowed to evolve made it a 'pressure point' for Pakistan over most of the countries in the region. For instance, the radical Wahabi-Sunni school of thought as perceived by the Taliban became an irritating factor for Iran. Similarly, secular-oriented Central Asian countries suddenly found that dissident movements in their respective countries were getting support from the Taliban. With the exception of Turkmenistan, all of them condemned Pakistan and the Taliban. The dissident movement in Chechnya was officially recognised by the Taliban, and dissident leaders like Zelimkhan were their guests. Even the sanctuary given to Saudi dissident leader Osama Bin Laden can be placed in this category.

Last, the Pakistan-Taliban failure to complete consolidation of their positions quickly rendered infructuous their success in restoring peace and order in the areas controlled by them. Some of their policies—especially against women—received considerable negative publicity resulting in a hardening of positions against them by the international community. The Taliban's method of ethnic cleansing narrowed their base, and in the international community's perception, they emerged as a Sunni Pushtoon-based group created by Pakistan to dominate the region. This automatically resulted in their being denied international recognition even though they exercise their authority over 80 to 90 per cent of Afghanistan. They are being bracketed as a state providing a training ground to radical elements from all over the Islamic world to resurrect a pan-Islamic world order.

However, this objective failed to materialise because the Taliban were not able to neutralise their opponents completely and establish their hegemony. In the process, many non-Afghan actors stepped in to pursue their own interests.

ISLAMIC ARMIES

Against this backdrop, the first issue that needs to be probed into is as to why Pakistan still persists with its surrogate, the Taliban. A number of explanations have been given by Pakistani commentators for this behaviour of Islamabad. They include: strategic depth against India in the event of an Indo-Pak war; and resolving the vexed issue of the Durand Line. These apart, an interesting dimension to the Pakistan-Taliban relationship was added by an Afghan journalist based in Peshawar (NWFP). According to Musa Khan Jalalzai:

> ... their (Pakistan's) goal was at once ideological and economic. Some (Pakistani armed forces) set their sights on detaching Central Asian Republics from the CIS, which they hoped would lead to disintegration of the Russian Federation itself and the emergence of a new space dominated by conservative Islamic regimes. From this point of view, the return to power of the neo-communists in Dushanbe, was a reversal for Islamabad, hence its support, through Afghanistan, for the Tajik rebels.[4]

On the economic level, Pakistan sought to make itself Central Asia's main route of access to the Indian Ocean. It, therefore, launched a

[4]Jalalzai, ibid., p. 195.

huge road construction programme in the summer of 1993 which was to link Karachi and the ports of the Indian Ocean with Central Asia via Peshawar and Afghanistan. According to Musa Khan, Maj. Gen. Naserullah Babar, Interior Minister in Benazir Bhutto's government, thought of two routes for Central Asia. 'If the route from Peshawar through Kabul, and the Salang Highway to Tashkent was blocked by war in Kabul, Pakistan should seek to open the western route, from Quetta through Kandahar and Herat to Turkmenistan.'[5]

If this objective of Pakistan is correct, it is operating on the assumption that having defeated the Red Army of the Soviet Union once, it is not difficult to defeat the disintegrated Soviet Union's armed forces once again. This also raises the question as to whether Pakistan is planning to convert its Taliban forces into a *jihadi* Islamic army. One can notice a particular pattern to this effect in the Pakistan-Taliban actions.

After giving support to Tajik rebels, the Pakistan-Taliban target has been Uzbekistan. The leadership of the Islamic Movement of Uzbekistan (IMU) attempted to assassinate Uzbek President Islam A. Karimov in February 1999 when six bombs in Tashkent killed 16 people and wounded 128. The leader of the IMU, Tahir Yoldassev, then fled to Taliban-controlled Afghanistan. In May 1999, the Taliban allowed Yoldassev to set up military training camps in northern Afghanistan, just a few miles from the Afghan-Uzbek border. Unconfirmed media reports say that he is training several hundred Islamic militants from Uzbekistan, Tajikistan and Kyrghistan, as well as Uighurs from Xinjiang Autonomous Region in China.[6]

Initially, the Taliban denied having extended any help to the IMU. But in June 1999, when the Uzbek government requested for the extradition of Tahir to Tashkent, it was rejected by the Taliban.

[5] *Ibid.*, p. 196

[6] Rashid, Ahmed. 1999. 'Talibanization?', in the *Nation* (Islamabad), 18 November.

In August 1999, another IMU leader, Juma Nanangani, entered southern Kyrghistan with about 800 militants, seized villages and threatened to invade Uzbekistan.[7] All this resulted in Uzbekistan severely condemning Pakistan for supporting dissident movements in Uzbekistan.

According to Ahmed Rashid, what brought in a new dimension was that

> ... although the IMU are not Deobandis, they are influenced by Wahhabism and have tried to impose the Taliban code in their areas of influence. Although the Uzbeks have historically been suspicious of the Pushtuns, the Taliban offer IMU a sanctuary from the Karimov crackdown with weapons, and the means to finance themselves through the drug trade.[8]

Iran is also uncomfortable by the advent of the Taliban. The Shi'ite regime in Teheran has long opposed the Pushtun-dominated Taliban's radicalism for two reasons. First, it is Sunni dominated; second it is a brainchild of Pakistan.

That the Taliban are virulently anti-Shi'ite is a well-documented fact. The way they massacred the Shi'ites in their war against their opponents in Herat and Bamiyan in 1998 and 1999 bears ample evidence of their bias against Shi'ites. In addition, Iranian support to anti-Taliban forces had been seen by the Taliban as an effort to confront them covertly by clerics in Teheran. Matters came to a head in August-September 1998 when the Taliban executed 11 Iranian diplomats in Mazar-e-Sharif. Iran threatened to invade Afghanistan, and war was averted by some quick diplomacy on the part of Pakistan.

Since then, the Taliban had been harbouring various Iranian dissident movements. They have given sanctuary to the relatively less

[7] *Ibid.*
[8] *Ibid.*

known Ahl-e-Sunnah Wal Jammat, made up of Sunni Iranians opposed to the regime in Teheran. The Taliban is also presumed to be entertaining leaders of the principal Iranian opposition group, the Iraq-based Mujahideen-e-Khalaq, in Kandahar. According to some reports, they have asked the Taliban for an operational base in Afghanistan.[9]

Chechnya is another example where the Taliban is trying to extend its influence. While the Russian forces are fighting Chechen rebel forces, the Taliban recognised Chechnya as an independent country on 16 February 2000. When a six-member delegation from Chechyna led by the republic's former President Zelimkhan Andarbayev called on the Taliban's supremo, Mullah Umar, along with recognition, it was announced that the Taliban authorities had allowed Chechen leaders to open a diplomatic mission in Kabul.[10]

Interestingly, after his visit to Kandahar the Chechen leader proceeded to Pakistan. In a meeting in Peshawar on 20 February 2000, Zelimkhan observed that Pakistan came into being in the name of Islam. Therefore, it should play a leading role in the Islamic ummah. 'It possessed [the] best armed forces with atomic technology and a stable economic system. In the light of these qualities, Pakistan could easily lead the Muslim world.'[11] Later, in a seminar in Islamabad on 23 February 2000, Zelimkhan pleaded for the creation of an International Islamic Force[12] to help Muslims in turmoil in different regions of the world. During this visit, Zelimkhan met important persons in the Pakistani government and discussed with them about granting recognition to Chechnya.

One can add to this list the Xinjiang Autonomous Region of the People's Republic of China. The Afghan heroin flooding Xinjiang

[9] *Ibid.*

[10] Yusufzai, Rahimullah. 2000. 'Taliban Recognises Chechen Govt.', *The News* (Islamabad), 17 January.

[11] Shahid, Shamim. 2000. 'Zelimkhan Urges Ummah to Establish Islamic Army', *The News*, 21 February.

[12] Jaidi, Javed. 2000. 'Zelimkhan Proposes International Islamic Force', *The News*, 24 February.

region is helping to fund the Uighurs and other Muslim ethnic groups to mobilise themselves against the authority of Beijing. In the 1980s, Uighur Muslims were trained in Afghanistan-Pakistan training camps to fight against the Red Army of the Soviet Union. This happened with the complete knowledge and approval of the authorities in Beijing. However, after the Red Army's withdrawal and the emergence of the Taliban in Afghanistan, Chinese security forces noticed that the arms and explosives used by the rebels came from Afghanistan and were being used against them. Though Taliban officials deny having harboured any Uighurs, some of the Uighur militants are known to be associated with Tahir Yoldassev and Osama Bin Laden.[13]

THE PAKISTAN-TALIBAN COMBINE

The next question is as to how the Pakistan-Taliban combine proposes to mobilise the needed manpower for this operation. Pakistan understands that it cannot commit its regular armed forces overtly for this 'Islamic Army': that would have serious repercussions internationally. The developments in all the Central Asian Republics and China indicate that the strategy that was adopted against the Red Army is being repeated. Pakistani planners perceive that they can launch a jihad and mujahideen can be mobilised from all over the Islamic world to fight these wars. According to one account, in the beginning (1982 to 1992) some 35,000 Muslim radicals from over 40 countries joined the Afghan jihad against the Red Army.

> Tens of thousands more came to study in Pakistani *madrassas*. Eventually more than 100,000 Muslim radicals were influenced by the Afghan *jehad*. The camps in Pakistan and Afghanistan where they were trained became virtual Universities promoting

[13]Rashid, *op. cit.*, n. 6 above. Also see: Aslam Khan, 2000, 'Angry China Forces Pakistan to Rein in the Taliban', *The News*, 19 February; Sreedhar, 1999, 'China, Taliban and India' in the *Deccan Chronicle* (Hyderabad), 9 June.

pan-Islamic radicalism in far off Algeria, Egypt, Sudan, the Philippines, Bangladesh and Yemen.[14]

With Saudi billionaire Osama Bin Laden coming on the scene in May 1996, things started happening fast with the Taliban. Within a span of four months of Bin Laden coming as a guest of Mullah Omar, the Taliban were able to capture Kabul. The following summer (May 1997), they were able to gain control of Mazar-e-Sharif, the last strong hold of anti-Taliban forces for three days. (26-28 May). This brought them recognition from Pakistan, the UAE and Saudi Arabia. Even though the Taliban suffered heavy losses in this mess in Mazar-e-Sharif, they made a fresh assault on it 15 months later and finally captured it in August 1998.

Though it is difficult to see a positive correlation between the arrival of Osama Bin Laden and the Taliban's advances, one can notice two significant developments in the attitude of the Pakistan-Taliban combine. The Taliban have started consolidating their position in the occupied territories much faster than they were doing the previous year. Equally interesting, the Taliban seem to be in a position to take any number of casualties, and are not having any problems with resources. Unlike in the past, there seems to be no scarcity of the basic necessities of life, specially food and transport facilities. None of the international agencies' aid workers operating in Taliban-controlled Afghanistan reported any starvation deaths in the past three years. This implies that the Pakistan-Taliban combine have ensured a subsistence-level economy to operate without any hindrance.

THE TALIBAN'S RESOURCES

That brings us to the last issue, as to how the Taliban is mobilising resources for these operations. Traditionally, Afghanistan is known as

[14]Rashid, *op. cit.*, n. 6 above. Also see Sreedhar and Ved, *Afghan Buzkashi, op. cit.*, n. 3 above.

an underdeveloped, backward economy. The problems were compounded by the 21-year-old civil war going on in the country. The Taliban is not in a position to bring in any large-scale organised economic activity because of the civil war. According to available evidence, the Taliban has three sources of income. The first is the narcotics trade. Since the Taliban captured Kabul, opium cultivation and production increased substantially. The UN Drug Control Programme estimates that in 1999, opium production in Afghanistan reached an all-time high of 4,600 metric tonnes (MT). This is more than double the estimated production of 2,100 MT in 1998.[15] The UNDCP also estimated that the area under poppy cultivation increased from 64,000 hectares in 1998 to some 91,000 hectares in 1999, and 97 per cent of cultivation occurred in Taliban-controlled areas.[16]

Table 1: Opium Gum Production in Afghanistan (1995-99)

Year	*Opium Gum (MT)*
1995	1,230
1996	1,230
1997	1,265
1998	2,100
1999	4,600

The Taliban collects a 20 per cent tax from opium dealers and transporters. This is supposed to be the main source of income for the Taliban. In 1999, with the opium price touching an all-time high in the international market (approximately US$75-80 per kg), the opium is supposed to have fetched over $100 million for the Taliban.[17] According to an Indian narcotics official, this is a

[15] 'Afghan Opium Production', on-line Centre for Afghan Studies, 31 March 2000. I am grateful to my colleague Dr K. Prabha for giving me some of her material on the drug trade.

[16] *Ibid.*

[17] Rashid, Ahmed. 2000. 'Flower Power', *The Nation*, 19 February.

conservative estimate. In his opinion, the Taliban collect at least three times more, and they must be collecting money from the mobile drug laboratories also.

In the past, Afghan drug lords used to export their opium and its products through Pakistan. However, this has changed from 1996 onwards, new routes have been added, which include Iran, other Persian Gulf states and Central Asia.[18] Ahmed Rashid, quoting US officials, says that with Osama Bin Laden's bank accounts frozen, he now finances his activities through opium money. Chinese officials report that drug smuggling from Afghanistan is similarly funding the Uighur opposition. The Uzbekistan government has drawn a direct drug-smuggling link between Afghanistan and Ferghana Valley where the IMU is based. The civil war in Tajikistan and Chechnya is funded by Afghan drugs. In other words, the drug-based economy of the Taliban is playing havoc with the economies of the region.[19]

Meanwhile, the smuggling of consumer goods, fuel, and foodstuffs through Afghanistan is wreaking further havoc. The contraband trade developed in the 1950s, when Pakistan granted landlocked Afghanistan the right to import duty-free goods through the port of Karachi under the Afghan Transit Trade Agreement (ATTA). Many of these imported goods were resold in Pakistani bazaars, but with the opening of Central Asia and Iran and the arrival of the Taliban in 1994, this trade has expanded enormously.[20]

Today, Afghan and Pakistani truckers smuggle goods across a huge swathe of territory that includes Russia, the Caucasus, Central Asia, Iran and Pakistan. The ATTA was worth only $50 million in the 1980s, but increased to $128 million in 1992-93 and then jumped to $266 million in 1994-95, the first year of the Taliban conquests. A 1999 World Bank study estimates that the smuggling trade between Pakistan and Afghanistan alone amounted to $2.5

[18] *Ibid.*
[19] *Ibid.*
[20] *Ibid.*

billion in 1997, equivalent to more than half of Afghanistan's estimated GDP. Add to that the smuggling to and from the rest of the region, and the total rises to $5 billion.[21]

This smuggling has crippled local industry in all the affected states, local factories cannot compete with smuggled, foreign-made, duty-free consumer goods. The smuggling also creates huge losses in customs revenue and sales taxes. According to Pakistan's Central Board of Revenue, Pakistan's losses in 1998 amounted to 30 per cent of the government's total revenues of $6 billion. The Taliban tax on the smuggling trade was its second-largest source of income after drugs. New transport and smuggling mafias have developed in Turkmenistan, Uzbekistan, Tajikistan and Iran. They are ignored by their governments, due to a web of corruption that benefits everyone from border guards to cabinet ministers. Not surprisingly, all these transport mafias are keen supporters and major founders of the Taliban. And this illegal economy is only expanding; Afghanistan's official one remains non-existent. The Afghan infrastructure is devastated, health care and education are virtually absent, and abject poverty is rampant. Afghanistan today has six working factories, compared to 220 in 1979. Fighting and smuggling offer the only employment.

The third source of money is international aid from various international aid agencies and donations from the fellow faithful in the Islamic world. Though no definite figure of the combined income from these sources is available, it would not exceed $50-60 million annually. This aid is largely used for feeding the urban population and maintaining some order in the living conditions. There is little chance of this money being diverted for the Taliban's policies of creating an Islamic army for their pan-Islamic ideology.

To sum up, Pakistan managed to create an outfit called the Taliban to achieve a number of objectives. In the process it managed to pursue two independent foreign policies: the official Pakistani

[21] *Ibid.*

foreign policy, and another based on jihad through the Taliban. Unfortunately for them, the international strategic community saw the linkages quite quickly. To add to the confusion, the Taliban started behaving erratically from the day of their inception. Each of the heterogeneous elements in the umbrella organisation of the Taliban started pursuing their own agenda. This automatically brought hostility from various quarters, making the whole idea vulnerable.

The Afghan mujahideen being replaced by the Taliban to complete the jihad initially received some enthusiastic support from various quarters. But as the Taliban started consolidating their position, it became clear to everyone that they were no better than their predecessors. In addition, *jihadi* warriors surfacing in various parts of the world and indulging in acts of violence and terrorism made everyone condemn this new phenomenon. In the last three years, the Taliban and mujahideen have become synonymous globally with violence, terrorism and ethnic cleansing. They can also be viewed as the nucleus of the Islamic army which is being articulated publicly by people like Zelimkhan with Pakistani patronage. The strategy being adopted for the creation of this new force may not sound good on paper, but it managed to mobilise a large number of people. In the past three years, they have confronted professional armies in three different places: on the Iran-Afghan border in August-September 1998, in the Kargil mountains of Ladakh region of J&K province of India in May-June 1999, and in Chechnya since December 1999. In the first two places, the Taliban/mujahideen retreated, and as things stand they may have to do so in Chechnya too.

This is no way should lead anyone to conclude that the Taliban/mujahideen are not a force to reckon with any more. In the name of guarding their faith, they are a highly motivated group. With better organisation and equipment, they may stage a comeback as they did at Mazar-e-Sharif.

But the strengths and weaknesses of this *jihadi* army must also be noted. They are restricted to Pakistan-Afghanistan. Their survival is dependent on the narcotics trade. The international community has already started exerting pressure on Pakistan-Afghanistan to close down these groups and their training camps. How far Pakistan and Mullah Umar will yield will be known in the coming months.

CHAPTER 3

Militant Islam: The Nemesis of Pakistan

Satish Kumar

The biggest irony of Pakistan's history is that Islam, which was supposedly the raison d'être *of Pakistan, not only failed to hold the country together, but also became the biggest source of its identity crisis. It is in the name of Islam that the country has suffered some of its worst internal conflicts in the last 10 years. And it is in the name of Islam that the country has created an image of being the most potent source of religious terrorism, which poses a threat to peace and stability in large parts of the world.*

The founders of Pakistan had set out to create a separate nation for all the Muslims of the subcontinent. But the number of Muslims who chose to stay back in India was more than the Muslims who opted to join Pakistan. Among those who joined Pakistan, 55 per cent decided to quit in 1971 to form a separate state. In 1974, under the prime ministership of Zulfikar Ali Bhutto, an influential section of Pakistani Muslims called 'Ahmediyas' was declared as non-Muslims, mainly on doctrinal grounds, i.e., differences on who constitutes a real Muslim. The last 20 years have witnessed accentuation of conflict between different Muslim sects, i.e., between Sunnis and Shias on one hand, and on the other between Sunnis themselves.

These political conflicts were manifestations of a deeper philosophical confusion as to what constitutes an Islamic state. History reveals no uniform pattern on which a religion-based state is structured. There is no uniformity even among the so-called Islamic states. Within Pakistan, the debate as to how the Islamic state of Pakistan should be structured, or what the role of Islam should be in this state, goes back to the days of its birth. While the ulema and the religious community in general were always keen that Islam should play a dominant role in Pakistan, they were never clear about what the role should be. Against this view, the modernists, i.e., the Western-educated political leaders, intellectuals, civil servants, and even the army officers in the first three decades wanted the Pakistani state to be run on Western parliamentary lines, with Islam playing a role only in the personal lives of the people.

Vigorous attempts at Islamicisation were made from the mid-1970s onwards, but all such attempts only sharpened the internal conflicts and contradictions in Pakistan, and did not make the people any happier. In the words of John Esposito, an astute scholar on the Islamic world, 'Islamization in Pakistan has travelled a rocky road.... Greeted with skepticism by some and with enthusiasm by many, the process thus far has led to frustration, disillusionment and opposition.... Pakistanis have found it easier to rally under the umbrella of Islam in opposition movements, e.g., against the British and Hindu rule or, more recently, against the Bhutto regime, than to agree upon what Islam and an Islamic state are.'[1]

ISLAM AND THE PAKISTANI STATE

In view of the fact that Pakistan was created in the name of Islam, it became imperative for the Pakistani leadership to lend some specific Islamic character to the Constitution of Pakistan. But this ran contrary to the requirement of making Pakistan a modern democratic state, the thinking in which the same Pakistani leadership had been brought up. Pakistan's constitutional history, therefore, has been one of struggle to make Pakistan a liberal democratic state on

[1]Esposito, John L. 1987. 'Islam: Ideology and Politics in Pakistan', in Ali Banuazizi and Myron Weiner (eds.), *The State, Religion, and Ethnic Politics: Pakistan, Iran, and Afghanistan*, pp. 360-1. Lahore: anguard Publishers.

one hand, and to make it conform as much as possible to Islamic orthodoxy on the other. In theory, the system that evolved by virtue of the 1973 Constitution provides enough scope for a liberal democracy to take root. In practice, however, civilian and military rulers with dictatorial tendencies used Islam as their tool. The result was that Islamist elements over the years acquired extra-constitutional power and influence disproportionate to their support among the electorate. This extra-constitutional power has become a major source of instability and disruption in Pakistan, and a threat to peace in the region.

The 1956 Constitution incorporated many elements of a modern parliamentary democracy (popular sovereignty, a party system, equality of all citizens) to which several Islamic clauses were added to respond to the demands of religious leaders. Among the principal Islamic provisions were: the state was to be called the 'Islamic Republic of Pakistan'; it was to be a democratic state based on Islamic principles; the head of state must be a Muslim; an Islamic research centre was to be established to assist in the 'reconstruction of Muslim society on a truly Islamic basis'; and there was a 'repugnancy clause' which stipulated that no law contrary to the Quran and *Sunna* could be enacted.

The 1956 Constitution was a compromise. The modernists got a document whose few Islamic provisions caused a minimum of inconvenience. The religious leaders wanted an Islamic state based on full implementation of the *Shariah*. They settled for a system in which no law could be repugnant to Islam. The relationship of modern constitutional concepts to Islamic principles was asserted but not delineated.

The rule of Field Marshal Ayub Khan (1958-69) provides another example of the failure to achieve a national consensus on the meaning, character, and implementation of Pakistan's Islamic ideology. Ayub Khan wanted to introduce modern, reformist Islam. He held the religious establishment chiefly responsible for the stagnant state of Islam, and, therefore, tended to ignore or minimise the role of the religious elite. Ayub Khan's Constitution of 1962 and the reforms embodied by him in the Muslim Family Laws ordinance of 1961 did not find favour with the religious leaders who saw in these steps a direct challenge to the traditional role of the ulema as the guardians of Islam, and advisers to the Muslim governments.

The 1962 Constitution generally adopted the Islamic provisions of the 1956 Constitution. There were, however, some significant changes. The new document initially omitted 'Islamic' from the official name of the republic, and the divine sovereignty phrase which limited the power of the state 'within the limits prescribed by Him'. Under strong pressure from orthodox sections, these Islamic provisions were restored by the First Amendment Bill of 1963. The issue of Muslim Family Law reform became a major point of contention between Ayub Khan and the religious establishment. In 1963, an attempt to repeal the new law was defeated in the National Assembly after some 20 hours of debate. Thus, during the first two decades of Pakistan's existence, the modernist elite succeeded in establishing a functioning state, but failed to evolve a consensus on what was needed to make Pakistan an Islamic state.

Ironically, it was the secularist Prime Minister Zulfikar Ali Bhutto, committed to the socialist goal of '*roti, kapda aur makan*' ('food, clothing and shelter'), who provided the maximum veneer of Islamicisation to Pakistani politics. Bhutto was compelled to do so because of a severe identity crisis faced by Pakistan after the secession of the eastern wing in 1971. Islam so far had failed to provide national cohesion. The effort was how to get the maximum out of it in future, particularly because strong ethnic sentiments were likely to assert themselves in residual Pakistan.

In a bid to establish a common identity with the Muslim world and draw closer to the Arab oil-producing countries for aid, Bhutto hosted an Islamic summit in Lahore in 1974. On this occasion, Col. Gaddafi addressed throngs of Pakistanis in Lahore, and President Sadat mediated between Pakistan and Bangladesh, leading to the latter's diplomatic recognition by Pakistan in the name of Islam.

At home, Bhutto introduced socialist measures like nationalisation of basic industries and land reforms and equated them with Islamic social justice. Phrases like *Musawat-i-Muhammadi* and *Islamic Musawat* became part of the Pakistan People's Party (PPP) rhetoric. In addition, in 1974, Bhutto yielded to the decades-long campaign of religious leaders to have the Ahmediyas declared as a non-Muslim minority. When Bhutto came under further pressure of a combine of Islamist parties called the People's National Alliance (PNA), which had declared his socialism as un-Islamic, Bhutto promised in his revised manifesto for the 1977 elections that he would have community life more firmly based on the Quran, and replace Sunday with Friday as the weekly holiday. Despite these strenuously Islamic endeavours of Bhutto, it was tragic that the downfall of this first directly elected government was brought about by the PNA, in collaboration with the military. This was the beginning of Islam acting as an ally of military dictatorship, and pitted against democracy. The future was to see much more of this alliance.

ISLAM AS AN INSTRUMENT OF DICTATORSHIP

Gen. Zia-ul-Haq set out to legitimise his military dictatorship in the name of Islam, and therefore cultivated and strengthened Islamist elements most vigorously. Claiming that he was going to establish *Nizam-i-Mustafa* ('the system of the Prophet'), or *Nizam-i-Islam* ('the system of Islam'), he took a number of steps. In a reconstituted Council of Islamic Ideology in 1977, he made provision for appointment of six ulema out of a total membership of 17. Three areas of immediate concern were picked up for Islamicisation of polity and economy, namely, the imposition of Islamic taxes, i.e., *zakat* (alms-giving) and *ushr* (agricultural tax); an economy free of *riba* (interest); and an Islamic penal code. In December 1978, Zia announced the creation of *Shariah* Benches, courts to determine whether or not existing laws were repugnant to Islam. In February 1979, as chief martial law administrator, Zia formally announced the creation of *Nizam-i-Islam*, and from then onwards imposed a series of Islamic measures affecting politics, laws, the courts, economics, education, culture, worship and women.

Paradoxically, however, the steps taken by Zia, despite the support of the Islamist elements, ended up in creating a series of conflicts and contradictions in Pakistani society and politics. Gen. Zia had postponed the promised elections in 1977 and 1979 on the ground that Pakistan's political system was not Islamic. These actions produced opposition not only from the supporters of Bhutto but also from PNA members who had supported Gen. Zia in toppling Bhutto. The constitution of *Shariah* courts came in for strong criticism from the legal profession as well as from women. The constitution of the *Majlis-e-Shoora* of 350 members in 1982 to serve as a federal advisory council until an elected national assembly was formed led to the consolidation of all democratic opposition under the name of the 'Movement for Restoration of Democracy' (MRD).

Zia's introduction of Islamic measures like *zakat, ushr*, and *hudood* punishments accentuated sectarian tension between the Sunnis and Shias. The Shias, who constitute nearly 25 per cent of the population, claim that their school of traditional legal thought, namely, Jafari *fiqh* is different in its prescription from the Hanafi-based Sunni *fiqh*. Shia demonstrations in 1980 against *zakat* had led to violence and bloodshed. Islamic resurgence under Zia brought to the surface the differences among various Sunni sects too, e.g., Deobandi, Barelvi, Wahabi, Ahle Hadith, and so forth.

Post-Zia analysts have held Zia-ul-Haq responsible for changing the nature and course of Pakistan's politics along dictatorial and fundamentalist-militant lines. According to a very perceptive analysis done by M. Ilyas Khan and Zaigham Khan, there were three elements in Zia's attitude towards politics.[2] First, he rendered politics

[2]'Zia and Politics: Attitude and Impact', *The Herald* (Karachi), August 1999, p. 54.

unworkable in Pakistan by blurring the distinction between politics and terrorism. By raising the bogey of Al-Zulfikar and conducting a massive propaganda campaign against terrorism, he hanged, flogged, and imprisoned pro-democracy political activists. Human rights organisations were branded agents of the West and hounded both by state functionaries and state-sponsored fundamentalists. Political parties were outlawed and local-body elections, the only ones permitted under Zia, were held on a non-party basis. At the same time, sectarian and other parties were reared in the provinces to fragment the polity, making it impossible for mainstream political parties to operate as effectively as they once did. Zia introduced institutionalised corruption by creating a non-party house (parliament) and dishing out hard cash to parliamentarians in the name of 'development funds'. The benefits from these funds never managed to trickle down to the constituents. This proved to be the single most important deathblow to politics, as the masses were increasingly convinced that, for most of their leaders, politics was just a wise investment.

Second, Gen. Zia proceeded to offer an alternative focus to the public in the shape of religion. A peculiar brand of Islam was created and packed specially for the purpose. Even Amir-ul-Azim, a member of the Jamaat-e-Islami, a beneficiary of power during Zia's regime, feels that 'terms like accountability, simplicity, clean government and Islamization were exploited by Zia'.[3]

In the words of Ilyas Khan and Zaigham Khan, 'In the new order (created by Zia), anything that was democratic was branded as un-Islamic which in effect meant that all political parties agitating for democracy found themselves battling a holy warrior instead of a military dictator.'[4] Student wings of religious parties were assigned the task of hounding out all leftist and pro-democracy elements from educational institutions. New laws such as the Hudood Ordinance were brought in to create an impression that Pakistan was

[3] *Ibid.*
[4] *Ibid.*

being turned into a truly Islamic state. *Salaat* committees were raised for door-to-door campaigning for *namaz.* Eating in public was strictly prohibited during *ramzan* [the month of fasting]. Religious programmes were allocated a disproportionate amount of time on the state-controlled Pakistan TV, and even textbooks were changed for more emphasis on religion.

Third, Gen. Zia altered the entire system of governance, apparently to ensure that even if politics did make a comeback, it would find no foothold in the new society. From a parliamentary democracy headed by an elected prime minister, he changed the system to an arrangement that later came to be known as 'the troika'. In this troika, the prime minister was only one of the three key decision makers, and often not the most powerful one. As Ilyas Khan and Zaighan Khan put it, 'The message was clear: any politician, even if he was elected to office, was not to be trusted and that there must exist mechanisms to keep him in check.'[5]

The use of Islam by Zia to justify and sustain his unconstitutional and dictatorial rule has been widely commented upon by writers and journalists in Pakistan. It has been pointed out that Zia-ul-Haq seized power under circumstances very different from those of Ayub Khan. At the time of Ayub Khan's coup, the people of Pakistan had not yet experienced a sustained period of democratic government. Therefore, 'developmentalism' sufficed as a tool of legitimacy for Ayub's regime. But Zia's coup followed a stint of elected government, the first ever in Pakistan's history. Therefore, Zia needed a new tool to legitimise the withdrawal of civil liberties by him. He chose Islam.

Zia employed Islam in affecting legislation as well as altering the character of state institutions such as the judiciary and the executive. For instance, the nominated *Majlis-e-Shoora* was given the semblance of a law-making body with wide-ranging powers. Since religion was made the point of reference for law-making, the stakes in sectarian

[5] *Ibid.*

interpretation of law increased. This caused the intensification of sectarian consciousness and deepening of sectarian cleavages. Islamicisation also precipitated further deterioration of the position of minorities. The minorities were already feeling insecure under the 1973 Constitution, which had declared Pakistan an 'Islamic state'. Zia further amended the constitution (Article 227) dividing the citizenry and its rights according to particular sects. Bhutto had already alienated the Ahmediyas by declaring them as non-Muslims through an amendment in 1974. Zia compounded the folly by declaring the profession and practice of the Ahmedi faith as 'criminal'. The addition of the blasphemy law to the penal code and the imposition of a separate electorate system intensified the division between Muslims and non-Muslims.

Thus, Zia's laws and policies resulted in making vast sections of the population extremely vulnerable to Islamic militancy. The pursuit of power through militant action by Islamic ideologues and their fundamentalist followers was encouraged by legislating in favour of such groups, and by the character of Zia's invocation of Islam. Hina Jilani, an eminent Pakistani commentator, has analysed the situation thus:

> The question here is not one of the interpretation of Islam, but of the motives and the context in which it was enforced: Zia did not employ Islam with the intention of inculcating positive values, such as peace and honesty, imbibed by Islam. His use of religion was limited to aggregating power with an authoritarian state through the police, army, and bureaucracy; exercising arbitrary control; and the denial of human rights to the Pakistani citizenry. Islam was enforced to deny women the right of being equal witnesses and to stifle freedom of expression, association, and even religion. A survey of laws and policies instituted by Zia reveals that Islam was invariably employed where rights were to be curtailed, and not for the expansion thereof.[6]

[6]'Zia and the End of Civil Society', *The Herald* (Karachi), August 1999, p. 63.

Zia-ul-Haq used Islam to promote his dictatorial rule but left behind a legacy of division, disruption, contradiction, and conflicts. It may be useful in this connection to recall here the views of one of the best Pakistani minds who also happens to be an important political leader, the former leader of the opposition in the Senate, Mr. Aitzaz Ahzan of the PPP. Answering a question on the future of Zia's legacy, he said:

> Personally, I see very bad times ahead. Within a matter of months, there will be a complete breakdown of civil society in Pakistan. The ethnic and nationalist forces in Sindh are confronting the state head on. The Punjab is becoming completely isolated because of the policies of Nawaz Sharif. There is going to be a reaction to the unfettered Punjabi dominance. The nationalist and ethnic groups will join together and the madrassas will erupt. The mujahideen returning from Kargil may add to the very uncertain and militarised situation. There will be a great civil conflict in the Punjab and the Frontier. The militants may not be able to take over the state apparatus, but civil society as we know it will be destroyed by fundamentalist and sectarian groups fighting each other.[7]

JIHAD AS A FOREIGN-POLICY TOOL

Pakistan used Islam as a conjunct of its foreign policy ever since its existence. This took the form of cultivating special relations with Muslim countries, receiving economic aid from them, establishing technological and military relationships with them, joining multilateral Islamic organisations and using their platforms to promote its foreign-policy goals, specially vis-à-vis India. In the last 20 years, however, Pakistan fell prey to the temptation of nurturing militancy in the name of Islam, and thought this to be an easy

[7]'Zia Replaced a Tolerant and Liberal Civil Society with an Intolerant, Retrogressive One'. Interview with Aitzaz Ahzan, *The Herald* (Karachi), August 1999, p. 61

option as a means of promoting its strategic goals in the region, particularly in Afghanistan and India. Pakistan called it 'jihad', which means 'holy war'. Obviously, the intention was to mobilise and motivate the Pakistan Army and irregular armed forces of all kinds in the name of Islam.

Pakistan first employed this strategy against the Soviet forces in Afghanistan from 1979 onwards. Pakistan should have been able to wage its war against the Soviet Union without invoking Islam. But by making it an Islamic cause, Pakistan found it easier to receive financial support from Saudi Arabia and volunteers from various Muslim countries. Countries like the United States and China, which supported Pakistan's 'Islamic' strategy merely because it was directed against the Soviet Union, are now reaping its bitter consequences. However, Pakistan thought that anti-Soviet jihad had served it well, and after the withdrawal of Soviet troops from Afghanistan in 1989, started adapting the same strategy to suit its requirements against India, in Jammu and Kashmir. Over the years, Pakistan and Afghanistan have become breeding grounds of *jihadi* forces which are being exported with the full backing of resource-rich Muslim countries to conflict zones like Bosnia, Kosovo, Chechnya, Dagestan, and to undertake specific terrorist missions against countries like the United States and India.

The story of Pakistan's involvement in the Afghan jihad against the Soviet forces is well known and extensively written about. Pakistan has no reason to deny this involvement. Also, it was the single largest beneficiary of it, in financial and political terms. But Pakistan chooses to be ambiguous about its involvement in post-Soviet Afghanistan, which has been afflicted with civil war ever since the Soviet withdrawal. Pakistan cast its lot with the Taliban, a force which grew out of Afghan refugee students who got their religious and military training in Pakistani madrassas and started making their impact on the battlefield from 1994 onwards.

Various accounts[8] would tend to suggest that Pakistan was directly responsible not only for the creation of the Taliban as a force, but also for their ideological and political motivation and their military training. Pakistan's objective could be to bring Afghanistan under the control of a friendly pushtun-dominated regime so that it could acquire strategic depth vis-à-vis India, have a safe transit route for Central Asian oil and gas pipelines, and get direct access to Central Asian Muslim republics for its long-term political, economic, and cultural goals.

Over the years, the western region of Pakistan and the southern region of Afghanistan became a vast network of training camps for highly motivated militant youth to perform assigned tasks in Afghanistan, and elsewhere in the world. Some of these camps, in the Khost region in southern Afghanistan, acquired publicity when the United States launched missile attacks on them in August 1998 in retaliation for Islamic terrorist attacks on the American embassies in Kenya and Tanzania earlier in the year.

A vivid account of the nature of these camps is available from the following investigative report of a Pakistani journalist:

> Militant and extremist Muslim groups from the Arab states, Pakistan, and Azad Kashmir, fighting against what they believe are the 'Westernized' regimes in their respective countries, and the Indian occupation of Kashmir, have found not just sanctuary in war ruined Afghanistan, but moral and material help as well. The presence of Arab and Pakistani nationals affiliated with different religious political parties and organisations on Afghan soil dates back to the Soviet invasion of Afghanistan in 1979. They were joined by Kashmiri freedom fighters in the late 1980s.

[8]For links between the Taliban and the Inter-Services Intelligence (ISI), see Ahmed Rashid, 'Pakistan and Taliban', in William Maley (ed.), 1998, *Fundamentalism Reborn? Afghanistan and the Taliban*, London: C. Hurst and Co., pp. 84-9. For the relationship between the Jamiat-ul-Ulema-I-Islam and the Taliban, see ibid, pp. 74-6.

At the inception of the Afghan war, Arabs hailing from Egypt, Saudi Arabia, Sudan, Algeria, Yemen, and other Muslim states, most of whom were members or sympathisers of the Egyptian-based Muslim Brotherhood (Akhwan-ul-Musalmeen), arrived in Afghanistan to fight the Soviets along-side the mujahideen led by former Afghan prime minister and chief of the Hezbe-Islami, Afghanistan, Gulbuddin Hekmatyar, A sizeable number of these Arabs, many of whom later joined ranks with other mujahideen factions, such as those led by the deposed Afghan President Burhanuddin Rabbani, Prof. Abdul Rab Rasul Sayyaf, and the chief of the Jamaat-ul-Dawa, late Maulvi Jamil-ur-Rehman, have now rallied under the banner of Osama Bin Laden.[9]

To understand the participation of Pakistani Islamic parties in these training activities and the deep links between them, the following part of the same report may be noted:

> Among the Pakistani and Kashmiri groups receiving training in Afghanistan to fight Indian troops in held Kashmir, are volunteers from the Harkat-ul-Mujahideen, an organisation which was carved out of the Harkat-ul-Ansar, a militant outfit declared a terrorist organisation by the United States. Harkat-ul-Ansar took over charge of the Salman Farsi training camp in the Jawar area after volunteers of the Hizb-ul-Mujahideen, a military wing of the Jamat-i-Islami, Pakistan, were evicted from Khost by the Taliban in 1996. The camps were then rechristened the Amir Muawiyya camp. The Harkat-ul-Mujahideen is led by Fazl-ur-Rehman Khalil of the Dera Ismail Khan district of the NWFP, and is apparently an independent organisation. Similar to this organisation is the Jamiat-ul-Mujahideen headed by Mufti Bashir, a splinter group of the Harkat-ul-Ansar based in Muzaffarabad, Azad Kashmir. Despite differences between them, both these groups shared the training facilities available at the Amir Muawiyya camp.

[9]'Afghanistan's Nation of Islam', *Newsline* (Karachi), September 1998, p. 37.

Another group that operates in the same area is the Harkat-ul-Jehad Islami, whose chief, Qari Saiful Islam Akhtar, was originally an activist of the Harkat-ul-Ansar but later parted ways with the organisation and formed his own group. Fighters affiliated with Akhtar's organisation have taken part in combat against Afghan opposition forces near Kabul. Interestingly, Qari Saiful Islam Akhtar is alleged to be one of the key characters in the conspiracy to overthrow [the] Benazir Bhutto government in 1995, and assassinate the top brass of the armed forces with an aim of bringing about an Islamic revolution in Pakistan. The two army officials involved in this coup attempt, Brigadier Mustansar Billah and Major Zaheer-ul-Islam Abbasi, were court martialed, but the chief of the Harkat-ul-Jehad Islami managed to escape justice by fleeing to Afghanistan.

A sizeable number of activists from the two factions of the Jamiat-e-Ulema-e-Islam led by Maulana Fazlur Rehman and Maulana Sami-ul-Haq respectively, have since 1994 also joined Taliban ranks. Reports also suggest that hundreds of volunteers of the Tehrik-e-Nifaz-e-Shariat-e-Muhammadi (TNSM) from the Malakand division have been sent to Afghanistan to strengthen Taliban ranks and receive military training. The participation of Jamaat-i-Islami workers in the Afghan jehad, especially the activists of its students wing, the Islami Jamiat-e-Taliba, is no secret. A number of them were killed in the battle between Gulbaddin Hikmatyar and Burhanuddin Rabbani for the control of Kabul.

This pan-Islamic band of holy crusaders has not restricted its activities to Afghanistan and Kashmir. Volunteers from assorted Arab groups, Pakistanis, and Kashmiris are reportedly also fighting alongside the Muslims in Chechnya, Bosnia, and recently Kosovo.[10]

[10] *Ibid.*, p. 38.

There is no dearth of evidence to suggest that Pakistan considers the Taliban as virtually an extension of its own military apparatus to jointly achieve the objectives of first capturing the whole of Afghanistan, then Kashmir, and then carry forward their jihad into the rest of India, and later beyond South Asia into Central Asia. A recent report in the *Far Eastern Economic Review* has the following to say:

> Pakistan's relationship with the Taliban is complex and fraught with severe repercussions for Islamabad. Mainstream Pakistani Islamic parties jostle for strategic alliances with the Taliban. Between 3,000 and 5,000 Pakistanis belonging to a dozen different Islamic fundamentalist parties are in Kabul with Islamabad's blessing for the Taliban summer offensive against the Northern Alliance.
>
> Their leaders have set up receiving centres and offices in the central district of Kabul, which now resembles a Pakistani suburb. Their presence has worrying implications for India-Pakistan relations. Some of these Pakistanis are war veterans from earlier Taliban campaigns and from recent fighting in Kashmir against Indian forces, while others are on summer holiday break from madrassas or Islamic schools.
>
> Also in Afghanistan, however, are the leaders of the Sipha-e-Sahaba Pakistan, or the SSP, and the Lashkar-e-Jhangvi—extremist Sunni groups accused of killing hundreds of Pakistani Shias and attempting to assassinate Prime Minister Nawaz Sharif... .
>
> The Taliban have also given sanctuary to fighters from Pakistan's Harkat-ul-Mujahideen, who have been linked to bin Laden and whom Washington declared a terrorist group last year for attacks on civilians in Bosnia, Chechnya, Indian-held Kashmir and Tajikistan.[11]

[11]'Afghanistan: Heart of Darkness,' *Far Eastern Economic Review*, 5 August 1999, pp. 11-12.

ISLAM, TERRORISM, AND SOCIETY

Imposition of Islam within the country and employment of jihad as a foreign-policy tool by Zia-ul-Haq led to strongly contradictory trends in Pakistani society. On one hand, the political appeal of Islamic parties declined sharply, as reflected in the decrease in the number of seats and percentage of votes won by them in successive elections. On the other, armed violence on account of sectarian conflicts increased many times; the number of religious, fundamentalist, and militant organisations, institutes, and madrassas went up dramatically; and more and more people, particularly belonging to the middle and upper-middle classes, were attracted towards the adoption of the '*pir-mazar*' culture, characterised by regular attendance at weekly meetings of organisations like the Tablighi-Jamaat.

The political appeal of religious parties started declining in the post-Bhutto period. From 20 per cent of the total votes cast in 1970, their share decreased to only 5.6 per cent in the 1993 election.[12] All religious parties put together held 18 seats in the National Assembly in 1970. The number came down to nine in the 1993 election.[13] The Jamaat-e-Islami won eight seats in the party-less polls of 1985. In 1993, this party could have only three of it members elected.[14]

There are many factors which are said to have been responsible for the decline in the political appeal of religious parties. First, the slogan of Islamicisation failed to attract public support because the Islamic identity of the country was never disputed. While religion was important to people, few of them wanted to see the country

[12]Adil, Adnan. 1996. 'Pakistan Politics: Emerging Trends and Issues'. Paper presented at an international seminar on 'Pakistan: Society, Economy and Polity' at the South Asia Studies Centre, Rajasthan University, Jaipur, 14-17 February, p. 5.

[13]See I.A. Rehman, 'Rout of the Mullahs', *Newsline* (Karachi), October 1993, pp. 44-6.

[14]Adil, *op. cit.*, n. 12 above, p. 5.

transformed into a theocratic state. Second, unlike in other Muslim countries such as Algeria and Egypt, Pakistan's Islamist groups remained allies of the military establishment. Their support for autocratic military rule caused serious damage to their political bases. Third, political support for Islamic parties deteriorated further when they became a part of the Islamic Jamhoori Ittehad. Another factor which affected the Islamic forces adversely was the emergence of militant sectarian groups like Sipah-e-Sahaba and Tehrik-e-Jafaria, Pakistan. These organisations divided the Islamic political forces and fuelled extremism.[15]

The rise of sectarianism is a phenomenon which is usually attributed to Zia-ul-Haq. But keen political observers in Pakistan believe that no ruler of Pakistan can be absolved of responsibility in this regard. According to I. A. Rehman, the sectarian virus 'was embedded in the religious trappings of the political demand for statehood in the form of Pakistan'.[16] Soon after Independence, the majority sect, the Sunnis, began to focus on the religious credentials of individuals enjoying authority in the political and administrative spheres. The presence of Shias in high positions was considered by the majority sect as an encroachment on power and privileges that it considered to be its exclusive preserve. Further, any manifestation of strength during the minority sect's rituals, such as *muharram* ceremonies and processions, drew an adverse reaction from the majority sect.

The Shia community was further antagonised—and protested vehemently—when the government tried to introduce religious courses in educational institutions. With the exception of Ayub Khan, every Pakistani ruler made concessions to theocracy, thereby fuelling sectarianism.[17] More than anything else, what acted as a

[15]For details, see Zahid Hussain, 'The Rise and Decline of Political Islam', *Newsline* (Karachi), February 1998, p. 44.

[16]Rehman, I.A. 'The Politics of Religion', *Newsline* (Karachi), October 1999, p. 78.

[17]For details, see *ibid.*, pp. 78-80.

catalyst to sectarian conflict was the raising of a large Sunni military force to capture Afghanistan from more indigenous claimants to power. The phenomenon of sectarianism could not be summed up more crisply than in the following words of I. A. Rehman: 'They (the Pakistani rulers) have paid no attention to the verdict of history that whenever and wherever politics has been made subservient to belief, a battle of sects has been unavoidable. All theocratic politics must inexorably degenerate into tyranny of the dominant sect.'[18]

Former Prime Minister Nawaz Sharif, a few weeks before his removal in the military coup of 12 October 1999, gave an unequivocal warning to the Taliban government of Afghanistan about providing sanctuary to Pakistani sectarian terrorists, following a fresh cycle of sectarian violence. This warning was an acknowledgement of the fact that the decades-long investment by Pakistan's secret agencies in Afghanistan had backfired, and the skills gained by militants in the use of explosives and light and heavy weapons were now being applied against its own people.

Pakistan can blame no one else for the backlash of its Afghanistan policy in terms of increased militancy and terrorism at home. Thousands of volunteers affiliated with the Jamiat-ul-Ulema-e-Islam (Fazlul Rehman) or JUI (F), Jamiat-ul-Ulema-e-Islam (Samiul Haq) or JUI (S), Tehrik Nifaz Shariat-i-Muhammadi, Sipah-e-Sahaba Pakistan, Lashkar-e-Jhangvi, and Kashmiri fighters from the Harkat-ul-Mujahideen, Hizb-ul-Mujahideen, Al Badr Mujahideen, and Arab nationals from different countries have been trained in guerrilla and defence warfare in Afghanistan during the last two decades, and hundreds more continue to report at the military camps in the Taliban-controlled areas of the country every month. What is noticeable about this activity is that no minimum age is set for the recruitment, and boys in their early teens are often seen heading for the frontline.[19]

[18]*Ibid.*, p. 80.

[19]See Behroz Khan, 'Sectarian Spill-over', *Newsline* (Karachi), October 1999, p. 76.

Giving an example of the impact of this cooperation between Afghanistan and Pakistan in the field of militancy and terrorism, Behroz Khan, a highly respected Pakistani journalist, points out in his report that the number of registered religious institutions in the NWFP, according to official statistics, is above 1000. There are no official estimates of other madrassas run by individuals in various parts of the province, Frontier and Tribal Areas (FATA), and the Northern Areas. According to conservative estimates, some 20,000 Afghan students are enrolled in various religious institutions in the NWFP and the overall strength of students at these seminaries is likely to be above 100,000. Officials in the country's security agencies believe that 15 to 20 of these religious institutions pose a potentially grave threat to law and order.[20]

The institutions for Sunni Muslims receive much of their funding from Saudi Arabia, and various NGOs and charity organisations from a number of Arab countries, in addition to a meagre amount provided from the *zakat* fund by the government. The Shia institutions, especially in the Kurram Agency, Hangu, and Peshawar districts, get their funding from Iran. The flow of unchecked foreign funding to both sects has allowed them to construct spacious mosques, *imambaras*, and religious institutions with boarding facilities. And the fallout of this heavy funding is the outburst of sectarian violence that leaves scores of the innocent dead—all in the name of religion.[21] In the words of Behroz Khan:

> Pakistan is thus paying a heavy price for its fundamentalist brigade's adventurism, both in terms of loss of precious human lives and in the threats it constantly faces from the world's powerful states of tough economic and military sanctions for its close ties with the Taliban government, and what are perceived as its links with terrorist networks.[22]

[20] *Ibid.*, p. 77.
[21] *Ibid.*
[22] *Ibid.*, p. 76.

The massive increase of sectarian violence in Pakistan in the last 20 years can thus be seen as the consequence of the Islamicisation policies of successive governments and the backlash of Pak-Afghan collusion in training the militants. It is, nevertheless, not easy to understand why the government and people of Pakistan have encouraged the establishment of such a large number of Islamic military organisations and groups in the last 10 or 15 years. The growth of such organisations continued unchecked even during the post-Zia democratic governments. A list of some of the largest Islamic militant organisations, provided by the *Herald* news magazine in September 1998, is as follows.

- Taliban.
- Harkat-ul-Mujahideen.
- Lashkar-e-Taiba.
- Hizb-ul-Mujahideen.
- Hizb-e-Wahadat.
- Sipah-e-Sahaba Pakistan.
- Lashkar-e-Jhangvi.
- Sipah-e-Mohammad Pakistan.[23]

The most typical of these organisations, and the one with the largest manpower and resources, is the Lashkar-e-Taiba ('army of the righteous'), even though it is the latest to join the ranks of the *jihadi* organisations. The Lashkar was formed after the Afghan jihad against Soviet occupation was nearly over, and is primarily meant to train recruits to do battle in Kashmir. There are many Pakistani *jihadi* organisations operating on the Indian side in Kashmir, but the Lashkar is the largest of them. The members of other *jihadi* organisations are mainly local men, assisted by fighters from the other countries such as Pakistan and Afghanistan. 'Eighty percent of the mujahideen in other jihadi groups operating in Kashmir come from that area', according to a spokesman of the Lashkar. 'But the

[23]For the antecedents and objectives of these organisations, see 'Allah's Armies', *The Herald* (Karachi), September 1998, p. 28.

case with Lashkar is exactly the opposite. Eighty percent of the Lashkar's soldiers belong to Pakistan', says the spokesman.[24]

Compared to other similar organisations, the Lashkar-e-Taiba has proved to be a resounding success. Since its inception, it has managed to attract thousands of committed young men to its fold. The Lashkar prefers not to reveal the exact number of men it deploys in Kashmir at a given time. 'The Amir decides how many mujahideen should be sent to the valley', is all that the spokesman reveals. 'The decision depends on the number of deaths that have taken place. It also depends on the requirement and capacity of the organisation inside Kashmir to absorb new fighters.'[25] What is known, however, is that the Lashkar recruits and trains many more men than it actually requires to fight in Kashmir at any given time.

An interview with the Amir of the Lashkar-e-Taiba reveals the specific motivations and goals of the organisation. An extract of the interview conducted by a Pakistani journalist, Zaigham Khan, with Hafiz Mohammed Khan, Amir, Lashkar-e-Taiba, runs as follows:

> There are Muslim organisations who preach and work on the missionary level inside and outside Pakistan, but they usually steer clear of jihad. However, not only has the need for jihad always existed, the present conditions demand it more than ever.
>
> Our jihad is confined strictly to non-Muslims, and particularly Hindus and Jews, the two main enemies of the Muslims. The Quran too has declared these two groups to be enemies of Islam. These two powers are creating problems for Muslims and for Pakistan. To my mind, Hindus are what the Quran terms as *mushriks* (polytheists). This Hinduism is the worst form of *shirk* (polytheism) in which 30 million gods are worshipped. And from here *shirk* has been smuggled to other nations of the world. Hindus are creating problems for us directly. If God gives us the

[24] See Zaigham Khan, 'Allah's Army', *The Herald* (Karachi), January 1998, p. 125.
[25] *Ibid.*

> power, we will enlarge the scope of jihad to include the Jews who are the worst danger for the Muslims.[26]

It may be pointed out here that the Lashkar-e-Taiba is the militant wing of Markaz-e-Dawa-wal Irshad, an Ahle Hadith Wahabi organisation based in Muridke, near Lahore. The Markaz was founded in 1987 by three university teachers, Zafar Iqbal and Hafiz Mohammad Saeed from the University of Engineering and Technology (UET) in Lahore, and Abdullah Azam of the International Islamic University. Azam was killed in a bomb blast in Peshawar in 1989, but both Zafar Iqbal and Hafiz Mohammad Saeed still teach at the UET and continue to lead the organisation. For the first three or four years, the Markaz was funded by Arab donors interested in 'purifying' Islam in the subcontinent, which is considered to have been tainted by the influence of Hinduism. But many Pakistani businessmen now support the Markaz generously, paying hundreds of thousands of rupees each month. The men who join the organisation also help to raise funds. The money has been used by the organisation to acquire precious land in Muridke. At the moment, the organisation runs 30 schools in which nearly 5,000 students are enrolled. 'We will continue to work in the twin fields of education and jehad', says Professor Zafar Iqbal, one of the founders of the Markaz. 'Jehad is carried out to establish the system of Allah in the world. But this system cannot be established without education', the professor explains.[26]

ISLAMIC MILITANCY AND PAKISTANI GOVERNANCE

Carried away by their successes in Afghanistan and by the clout acquired by them through militancy within Pakistan, the Islamic parties have of late started pressurising the governments in Pakistan on matters of domestic and foreign policy, making their already not-

[26] *Ibid.*, p. 125.

too-easy task still more difficult. For instance, on 14 September 1998, Qazi Hussain Ahmed, the Amir of the Jamaat-e-Islami, while addressing a protest rally against the Comprehensive Test Ban Treaty (CTBT) in front of the parliament building in Islamabad, thundered: 'You will dig your graves by signing the CTBT. You will sign your death warrant by doing so, and we will take out your funeral procession from the National Assembly.'[27]

The qazi was not alone in his condemnation of the government's dithering' on the CTBT issue. Equally incendiary views were being expressed by numerous religious organisations across the country. The very next day, Maulana Samiul Haq's Darul Uloom Haqqania, one of the most influential Deobandi madrassas in the country, issued a fatwa deeming any support for the CTBT, whether verbal or in writing, to be rebellion against the Quran and *Sunna*. The fatwa ostensibly came in response to a query in which the petitioner, after arguing that the government would be 'selling out to the Jewish, Christian, and Hindu powers and dealing a fatal blow to the forces of jihad' by signing the CTBT, had posed the question: 'Does the government have the right to sign this death warrant, this document of shame?'[28]

What explains so much bravado on the part of Islamic organisations that they venture to express opinions and incite the masses on issues on which they have little knowledge, and which are not directly related to their original purposes? The only plausible explanation is that ever since the creation of Pakistan, the ruling elite, which includes the army, the bureaucracy, the political class, and consequently the people of Pakistan, have allowed themselves to be held hostage to the belief that since Islam was the only justification for the creation of Pakistan, it is in the name of Islam alone that

[27]See Zaigham Khan, 'Playing with Fire', *The Herald* (Karachi), September 1998, p. 25.

[28]*Ibid*, p. 26.

Pakistan can be held together. And this, despite the warning given by Quaid-e-Azam Muhammad Ali Jinnah in his speech in the Constituent Assembly on 11 August 1948 that the political role of Islam was over after Pakistan had been achieved.

Since the Pakistani elite failed to discover alternative sources of inspiration to sustain and strengthen the country, it fell back on Islam and its 'proprietors' after every shock that the country received from within or without, giving to these 'proprietors' a sense of importance disproportionate to their political worth. The process culminated in a symbiotic relationship between Islamic political parties and various militant outfits that came into existence during the anti-Soviet Afghan jihad, with disastrous consequences for Pakistan itself in the post-Soviet period.

For instance, the Jamiat-ul-Ulema-e-Islam (JUI) has a fundamental connection with the Taliban, since the rank and file of the student militia was originally formed by Afghans educated at JUI-run madrassas. The Sipah-e-Sahaba is also linked to the Taliban, as well as to the Harkat-ul-Ansar. The Jamaat-e-Islami is said to have spawned a guerrilla offshoot, the Hizb-ul-Mujahideen, while most Ahle Hadith political groups in the country are affiliated with the Lashkar-e-Taiba. Similarly, Shia political parties in Pakistan are associated with the Hizb-e-Wahadat. 'After cutting their teeth in battle in Afghanistan and Kashmir, the young Islamist militants prove to be a key human resource for hard-line religious parties in their activities on the streets of Pakistan.'[29] Together, the Islamic political parties and the militant outfits have given rise to what may be called a '*jihadi* culture', with *jihadi* movements and *jihadi* strategies which are deployed inside and outside the country by vested interests. The consequence, in terms of instability, disruption, disaffection, conflict, and contradiction, within Pakistan and outside, is there for anyone to see.

[29] *Ibid*, pp. 26-7.

CONCLUSION

Pakistan has been described by many in the West and some in Pakistan as a 'failed state'. In the words of Syed Ali Dayan Hasan, a distinguished Pakistani commentator:

> Pakistan is indeed a failed state. A state that does not have enough self-confidence to take criticism can only be described thus. A state that feels constrained to legalise bigotry and exclusion, extremism and prejudice, coercion and oppression in order to survive is certainly not presiding over a vibrant, successful and self-assured society. When mediocre opportunists start looking and sounding like heroes, it is time to unequivocally condemn those whose venality is responsible for the moral schizophrenia enveloping society. The responsibility for this situation ultimately rests with the failing leaders of Pakistan. Sharif is not just one of them—he may well be the worst of them.[30]

For India and the rest of the world, the question is not whether Pakistan is a failed state. Even if it is a failed state, it cannot be wished away. The relevant question is: What does Pakistan mean to the rest of the world? Is it a source of stability and strength, or a source of disruption caused by terrorism and militancy of which Pakistan has become a major breeding ground? The culture of terrorism and militancy, the so-called '*jihadi*' culture, supposedly sanctified by Islam, has already done enough damage to Pakistan itself, so much so that self-respecting Pakistanis feel embarrassed and ashamed. It is for the rest of the world to see whether it can help Pakistan put itself on an even keel, in terms of values and principles, and meanwhile guard itself against the adverse repercussions of a 'failed state', ideologically speaking, at least.

[30]Hasan, Syed Ali Dayan. 1999. 'Failing Leadership in a Failed State', *The Herald* (Karachi), June 1999, p. 43.

CHAPTER 4

Political Dimensions of Jehad

Kalim Bahadur

The terrorist attacks on the Twin Towers of the World Trade Centre on 11 September 2001 has exposed the real nature of the jehad as practiced by the radical Islamic fundamentalists. The attack led to the death and injury to thousands of people in the two cities. It is now known that the attacks were the handiwork of Osama bin Laden and his al-Qaida organisation. Osama bin Laden had been given refuge by the Taliban in Afghanistan. They have been patronised by the successive regimes in Pakistan particularly by the military government of General Musharraf. Pakistan failed to recognise that the militant groups were dangerous gangs whose resources and reach continued to grow till they were able to launch the attacks on New York and Washington. The United States has planned to retaliate with their massive military power against the international terrorist network in Afghanistan and elsewhere and its leader Osama Bin Laden. The adventurist action by the terrorists would bring untold sufferings to the people of Afghanistan and may even embroil many other countries into the vortex of war and bloodshed.

CONCEPTUALISATION OF JEHAD

The word jehad is derived from *Juhd* which signifies exertion, striving and endeavour and ceaseless efforts to one's utmost capacity bestowed by Allah. It is also used in the sense of exerting one's power and ability without implying any sense of war. In the language of Shariah this word is also used for war (*jehad-bis-Saif*), with the object of bringing end to oppression and aggression against Islam. Its object is not to propagate Islam, but to remove those tyrannical forces which are inimical to Islam and are not prepared to give a fair deal.[1] Jehad has two possible definitions: the greater, which is the spiritual struggle of each man, against vice, passion and ignorance. Imam Ghazali has also in his classical text on Jehad *al Nafs* focused on this aspect of the concept of jehad. According to Ghazali, *Nafs* has two meanings, one, power of anger and sexual appetite in human beings; two, soul i.e., human being in reality, his self and his person. This understanding of jehad has been presented by apologetics of modern times, but is an understanding of the term rarely used by Muslims themselves. Jehad means struggle against oneself to overcome evil and also in the cause of Islam. It makes no reference to warring. Classical jurists have classified many forms of jehad, but broadly it has been divided into two. One, *al-jehad-ul-akbar*, the greater jehad which means exerting oneself against temptations and evil; two, *al-jehad-ul-asghar*, or lesser jehad which means fighting in the path of God. The interpretation that some preachers of modern *madrasas* have given in the recent times is at complete variance with the Quranic text.[2] It is claimed that the lesser jehad is simplified to cover holy war against infidels and infidel countries. This kind of jehad is described in both the Holy Quran and in the *hadiths*. It is also stated that the Muslim law has divided the world into two entities, *dâr-ul-Islâm*, the abode of Islam, and *dâr-ul-harb*, the abode of war. Battling against the abode of war was a duty for a Muslim, as this is the only way Islam could replace the warlike conditions of the infidels' society with peace. Jehad can be both defending against or attacking an enemy.

There are differences among the Islamic scholars about the meaning and understanding of jehad. Jehad is usually misconstrued as war, with all its connotations of violence and bloodshed.

[1]Dawn; 19 January 2001

[2]Rafiq Zakaria; 'This Blood Won't Wash'; *The Hindustan Times*; 23 August 2001

However, in the Islamic context, and in the literal sense, the word jehad simply means a struggle—doing one's utmost to further a worthy cause. The actual Arabic equivalent of war, is *qital*, and even this is meant in a defensive sense. Many people think that it is synonymous with war (*Qital*) undertaken for spreading Islam. Even a number of the Ulema cannot discern the distinction between *qital* and jehad as laid down in the Quran. Many western scholars also use the term war for jehad.[3]

The concept of jehad has figured as the core of Islamic strategic thinking throughout the history of Islamic world. The Quranic concepts of war have been open to different interpretations by scholars through the centuries. Many contemporary scholars have written extensively on the concept and meaning of jehad. The founder of the Jamaat-e-Islami of Pakistan, Maulana Abul Ala Maududi (1903-1979) produced a voluminous work titled *al jehad fil Islam*, which was published in 1930. It covered a wide field which included an analysis of the Islamic concepts of jehad, defensive war, tactical war, the spread of Islam by sword, and the Islamic laws of war and peace.[4] If Maududi shares anything with other fundamentalists it is the emphasis on the jehadi 17 paradigm, the belief in jehad as a means to achieve the Islamic state. The most significant type of jehad is the use of violence as an element of general strategy.[5] Jehad is another name for the attempt to establish divine order; the Quran therefore, declares it to be the touchstone of belief. In other words it is total struggle, offensive or defensive as the need be, against the usurpation of God's sovereignty, whether by pseudo-religious monarchists or westernized secular elements.[6]

[3]Leonard Binder: Religion and Politics in Pakistan: 1961: Berkeley: University of California Press p. 153.

[4]Sayyid Ali Naqi; *Sayyid Maududi ka Ahd*; Lahore; Al Badr Publications; 1980; pp. 19-20.

[5]Sohail Mahmood; *Islamic Fundamentalism in Pakistan, Egypt and Iran*; Lahore; Vanguard Books Ltd; 1995; p. 112.

[6]Martin E Marty and R.Scott Appleby; *Fundamentalisms Comprehended*; Chicago; The University of Chicago Press; 1993; p.310.

The religious duties of the Muslims centre on the five pillars of Islam. They are *Kalma* or the recital of creed, *Salat* or five daily prayers, *Roza* or fasting during Ramzan, *Zakat* or alms giving and lastly *Haj*, pilgrimage to Mecca. It has been asserted that the importance of jehad ranks next only to *Namaz* (ritual prayers), *Roza* and *Haj*.[7] However, only one Islamic sect has declared jehad as the sixth pillar of Islam, namely, the Kharijites who were responsible for the killing of Hazrat Ali, the fourth Caliph, cousin and son-in-law of Prophet Mohammad.[8] One example of jehad was the movement led by Sayyid Ahmed Barelvi which was aimed at the establishment of an ideal Islamic state in India. The movement, however, ended in defeat and the death of Sayyid Ahmed Barelvi (1781-1831). According to one view jehad ignores the ABC of war according to Clausewitz. Although the scale is larger than that of the vendetta or the revolt, jehad brings no innovation in tactics or strategy, but only in references of legitimation. Jehad, in fact, knows no political space, no state. Its space is that of the *Umma*. Jehad knows no borders. The state is the provisional incarnation of the Muslim nation (*Millat*); in reality, it exists only in crisis and is not institutionalized.[9]

According to Muhammad Iqbal, jehad was not an offensive attack of the Muslim community for self aggrandisement. All wars waged under the leadership of Prophet Muhammad were defensive. He claimed that while defensive wars are permitted, aggressive warfare is contrary to the Quran. Iqbal believed that any attempt at social change through employment of violence is impossible.[10] These views of Iqbal and Maududi diverge significantly from those of Sayyid Qutb (1906-1966), one of the ideologues of the Muslim

[7]Aziz Ahmed; *Islamic Culture in the Indian Environment*; Delhi; Oxford University Press; 1999; p. 214

[8]Jamal Ahmed Khan, 'War Is Not the Aim of Jehad'; *The Times of India*; 22 September 2001

[9]Oliver Roy; *The Failure of Political Islam*; Cambridge; I.B. Tauris; 1994; p. 154

[10]John Esposito; 'Muhammad Iqbal and the Islamic State'; in John Esposito; *Voices of Resurgent Islam*; New York; Oxford University Press; 1983; pp. 181-82.

Brothers (*Ikhwan al Muslimeen*) of Egypt. His views exercise considerable influence over the militant movements which are active in many countries of the Islamic world. Qutb claims that Islam rejects all justifications for war such as nationalism, racism, greed, and economic expansion. But then he says, Islam must be guaranteed freedom of propagation otherwise Muslims can go to war against those who put obstacles in their way. Qutb says that Islam confronts those forces which impede its progress. According to Qutb, war against those forces is justified who do not accept Islam or those who refuse to pay the tax (*jiziya*). None of these ideologues, however, would agree to allow the same freedom of propagation to those of other religions in their Islamic states. Qutb claims that jehad is an essential characteristic of Islam commended by the Quran and that the Muslims should not be embarrassed by it or renounce it.[11] Qutb believed that prevailing conditions in a particular country be viewed as having no impact on the practice of jehad, the understanding of which he believed had been corrupted by the writings of the orientalist scholars. Jehad is itself the process of purification of the world in pursuit of the *Din*. It was not meant as a defensive measure in the face of aggression from those who opposed Islam but as a vital process in which Muslims should take the initiative as divinely given right to step forward and establish political authority, so that they may establish the divine system on earth while leaving the matter of belief to the individual conscience.[12]

Some contemporary *jehadis*, for example those who are now fighting in Jammu and Kashmir, claim that jehad can be waged even if there is no Islamic state and in that case jehad can be waged by the people on their own.[13] One of Pakistan's major jehadi institution,

[11]Yvoune Y. Haddad; 'Sayyid Qutb: Ideologue of the Islamic Revival', in Ibid; pp. 84-85

[12]Mark Huband; *Warriors of the Prophet; The Struggle for Islam*; 1999; Boulder, Colorado; Westview Press; p. 89

[13]Zaigham Khan; 'Allah's Army'; *Herald*; Karachi; January 1998; pp. 123-133

the Markaz-e-Dawa-wal-Irshad, was set up in 1987 to combine two primary missions of Islam preaching and jehad. Their concept of jehad is that it can be declared even if there is no Islamic state. They believe if an Islamic state existed it would be its responsibility to wage jehad but if there is no Islamic state then they have to do it on their own. They claim that Muslims are backward not because they have lagged behind in education, science and technology but because they have given up jehad and therefore, science and technology have passed into the hands of non-Muslims. All *jehadis* are against democracy. They have also devised reasons for this. Democracy according to them was inherited from alien governments. These are (democratic) all useless practices and part of the system against which they are fighting. It is not possible for them to work under democracy and establish the Islamic system.[14] One noted Indian Islamic scholar has a contrary view and says that according to his understanding of Islam only a state or government can wage a jehad. And before doing that a declaration has to be made that it is at war. Even during war, only military, not civilians are to be targeted. Moreover, according to him Islam does not sanction aggression, it only allows retaliation. He makes an interesting point that in Islam you get killed in jehad and not court death, which is what many terrorists seem to be doing.[15] According to a sociologist the emphasis on martyrdom and jehad have acquired a new meaning. They no longer emphasise dying for a cause as much as killing for a cause. Killing for a cause takes away from the singularity and purity of martyrs dying to uphold a cause against a powerful enemy. Instead it is important now for suicide terrorist squads to go out in a blaze of glory taking down a lot of other people with them.[16]

The concept of jehad has been evolved by the modern Islamists to such an extent where even standing armies of *jehadis* are being

[14] *Ibid.*

[15] Maulana Waheeduddin Khan in *The Hindustan Times*; 16 September 2001

[16] *Times of India*; 25 September 2001

trained. Pakistan has tens of thousands of *madrasas*. Often the students learn only the Quran. They will not be taught much maths and probably no science or literature or any other secular subject regarded in the West as important for functioning in modern society. Many of these schools preach jehad with varying degrees of militancy. Pakistani officials estimate that 10 to 15 percent of the country's *madrasas* promote extremist ideologies. Mujeebur-Rehman Inqalabi, a leader of Pakistan's Sunni sectarian party, Sipah-e-Sahaba, claims that the United States had finally figured out that *madrasas* comprise the base for jehad and was, therefore, pressurising Pakistan to shut them down. He asserts that this is not possible since the '*madrasas* are the supply line for jehad'. Where the state controls *madrasas*, as in Egypt and Jordan, the voices for jehad have been silenced.[17] Pakistan and Afghanistan are now the only countries where it is possible to preach jehad in the schools. The terrorist activities in America, like the World Trade Centre bombing some years ago and the terrorist attack on the Twin Towers of the World Trade Centre on 11 September 2001 and Mir Aimal Kansi's attack at the CIA, are a reaction to the US attempt to impose a new world order on the rest of the world. He asserts that America is trying to crush jehad, but this will only exacerbate the situation.

Whatever might have been the justification for jehad in its original conception in the Quranic revelation, it had a different meaning and significance in the Middle Ages and has a different one in modern times. The theory of jehad may well be exploited for military and political expansion and there may be economic motivations behind it.[18] A deeper historical analysis will no doubt reveal that it is doubtful if any one of the invasions of India about eight or nine hundred years ago were purely religious invasions undertaken by religious fanatics or by enthusiasts wanting to spread

[17]Jessica Stern; "Pakistan's jehad Culture"; *Foreign Affairs*, (New York); Vol.79 No. 6; p. 119

[18]Ahmed; n. 7; p. 78

Islam. Like all conquests they were actuated by temporal and material motives rather than by religious zeal.[19]

The hardline aggressive interpretations of the Quranic concepts of jehad have been opposed by several theologians and scholars. According to Imam Raghib the Quranic lines relating to jehad mean three types of jehad; first, to face the enemies of Islam; second, to fight against oneself, (to control selfish desires); third, to strive towards the path of God with one's life and wealth. Another scholar has opined that the concept of jehad signifying the waging of war is a post-Quranic usage.[20] Some writers have also claimed that Islam relies on persuasion and other peaceful means of expansion as against Qutb's interpretation and jehad is allowed only for self defence or for support to a defenceless ally. Iqbal's assertion that all the wars waged by Prophet Mohammad were defensive, points to his understanding of the defensive nature of jehad.[21]

Maulana Abul Kalam Azad, the renowned Indian Islamic scholar had said that there are serious misconceptions regarding the real meaning of jehad. Many people think that jehad means only to fight. The critics of Islam too labour under this misunderstanding, whereas to think thus is to utterly narrow the practical scope of this sacred commandment. Jehad means to 'strive to the utmost'. In the Quran and Sunna terminology, this utmost exertion, which is undertaken for the sake of truth rather than personal ends, is indicated by the word 'jehad'. This effort could be with one's life, or property, or expenditure of time, or by bearing labour and hardship, or fighting the enemy and shedding blood.[22]

In his great English work on jehad published in 1884, the famous rationalist religious scholar, Maulavi Charagh Ali, wrote,

[19] *Ibid*; p. 78-79

[20] Asghar Ali Engineer; *Islam and the Concept of jehad*; Mumbai; Institute of Islamic Studies; 1998; vol. no.1; no.10. p. 2

[21] *Ibid*; p. 21

[22] Abul Kalam Azad; Mas'ala Khilafat; p; 47 www.tariq.bitshop.com/misconceptions/jehad/jleders.htm

"Jehad does not mean the waging of war; I do not mean to contend that the Quran does not contain injunctions to fight or wage war. There are many verses enjoining the Prophet's followers to prosecute a defensive war, but not one of aggression. The words *qatal* and *qital* distinctly indicate this".[23]

PAKISTAN AND JEHAD

Islamic militants in the Middle East and Afghanistan are well-known but very little is known, about those in Kashmir perhaps because they operate mainly in the Indian state of Jammu and Kashmir and do not pose a terrorist threat outside South Asia. General Musharraf, Pakistan's military ruler, calls them 'freedom fighters' and admonishes the West not to confuse jehad with terrorism. Musharraf is right about the distinction-the jehad doctrine delineates acceptable war behaviour and explicitly outlaws terrorism-but he is wrong about the militant group's activities.[24] It may be remembered that the summit meeting between the President of Pakistan, General Musharraf and the Prime Minister of India Atal Behari Vajpayee held at Agra in July had collapsed on the issue of the terrorists in Kashmir whom the General insisted on calling 'freedom fighters'.

Kashmir has been the focus of India-Pakistan tensions and conflicts ever since independence in 1947. They have fought three wars and during the rest of the period their relations have been tense often degenerating into virtual war. Pakistani leaders have been calling the Kashmir issue as an unfinished agenda of the partition of India. It was as early as October 1947 that Pakistan, soon after the independence of India, had refused to recognise the accession of the Kashmir state to the Indian Union and had sponsored the first invasion of the state by the Pathans from the tribal areas of the North-West Frontier Province of the country. The Pathan invasion, which was soon joined by the Pakistan's armed forces was called a

[23]Chiragh Ali; Jehad; 1977; Karachi; 1977; p. 192.
[24]Ibid; n. 17; p. 119

jehad by the Pakistani leaders. The issue of the accession of Kashmir to the Indian Union was one of the many economic and political disputes which were the consequence of the complexities of the process of the partitioning of the Indian subcontinent by the British rulers, which later became the cause of conflicts between the two countries. The Pakistani rulers claim that the war in Kashmir was a jehad was accepted by most *Ulema* in that country, but there were also some who had their doubts about the strict interpretation of the Islamic texts. Among the first to raise objections was the founder of the Jamaat-e-Islami of Pakistan, Maulana Abul Ala Maududi.

Maududi faced the problem of reconciling whether the Pakistani war in Kashmir was jehad in the early months after Independence. In May 1948 during a local gathering of the Jamaat-e-Islami in Peshawar, the publicity officer of the Pakistan occupied Kashmir government asked the Maulana why he did not participate in the jehad in Kashmir. The Maulana replied that if the Government of Pakistan openly declared jehad or war, he would fight in the front ranks. Moreover, Pakistan had not as yet been declared an Islamic state. He did not consider it Islamic morality that while the Pakistani armed forces were fighting secretly they declared they were not fighting. Maududi later further clarified his position. According to him his stand was based on the Quran and he quoted the appropriate verses. He said that if Muslims were oppressed outside the country's borders they could be helped, provided there were no agreements with the country oppressing them. In case of such agreements no belligerent activities could be undertaken against that country.[25] It may be remembered that in early May 1948, Pakistan had not admitted that its armed forces were fighting in the Indian state of Jammu and Kashmir, that admission came later. Incidentally the Kargil operation in the summer of 1999 by the Pakistan armed forces was only a repeat of the same policy. Pakistani rulers have yet to admit that it was their Northern Light Infantry which was fighting in Kargil.

[25] *Tarjumanul Quran*; Lahore; vol. 31, no. 2.p. 121

In fact, in the late forties Maududi made two points; first, that Pakistan was not yet an Islamic state and therefore, it could not declare a jehad; and second, that there should be no subterfuge about the jehad. Maududi later changed his stand on the Pathan invasion being a jehad. He then argued that after the passing of the Objective Resolution in March 1949 by the Constituent Assembly, Pakistan had become an Islamic state in the making and hence it could give a call for a jehad.[26] It was a typical example of the *Ulema's* convoluted reasoning for changing their views on important Islamic issues on which they had earlier taken a different stand. Maududi did this volte-face several times during his career. What then is the definition and the concept of jehad in Pakistan?

It is claimed by one viewpoint that Jehad could only be declared by an Islamic state. One of them was Maududi, but some of the modern *jehadis* assert that even individuals could declare jehad. Could Pakistan declare jehad? Maududi had resolved his problem using the pretext of The Objective Resolution. At that time the question was whether Pakistan was an Islamic state? The phrase 'Islamic state' did not figure prominently during the period of struggle for Pakistan. It is true that the concept of an Islamic state was not seriously mooted on the intellectual plane, nor cogently and explicitly defined by the leader Mohammad Ali Jinnah, nor by other leaders of the movement. Islam, according to Jinnah was to be the guiding principle of the new state in the most generalised way, which, however, was never spelt out by him.[27] There was never any attention paid to the political system nor to the security concerns of the new state in the higher echelons of the Muslim League leadership. Keith Callard had remarked about the question of the Islamic state in Pakistan that "the great debate that might have done justice to the price and crucialty of Pakistan never really happened ... Pakistan emerged from the welter of circumstance and propaganda,

[26]Binder; n. 3; p. 153

[27]Sharif Al Mujahid; *Quaid-I-Azam Jinnah; Studies in Interpretations*', Karachi; Quaid-I-Azam Academy; 1981; pp. 229

and multitude of words, without its ultimate *raison d'etre* ever receiving the quality of conscious and spiritual determination which its magnitude deserved. The strangest fact is that so little about ultimate Islam went into its official apology."[28]

Sharif Al Mujahid, who was the head of the Quaid-i-Azam Academy argues that Jinnah was a political leader and not a systematic thinker, a leader of men rather than of thought, a (political) realist rather than a visionary. This clarification was offered to explain away Jinnah's speech at the inaugural session of the Constituent Assembly of Pakistan on 11 August 1947 where he had put forth the idea of almost a secular state for Pakistan.[29] How could a Pakistan of Jinnah's conception, spelt out by him at the first meeting of the Constituent Assembly of Pakistan, declare jehad? Moreover, Pakistan's division into two wings, a thousand miles apart, would have formidable strategic problems, did not find any reflection is his concerns. It was Mohammad Iqbal (1875-1938) who had in his address to the Allahabad session of the Muslim League in 1930, while discussing his proposal for the creation of an autonomous Muslim state in the north-west of India, had suggested that "the North-West India Muslims will prove the best defenders of India against a foreign invasion be the invasion one of ideas or of bayonets".[30] Iqbal's view had found an echo in some Pakistani security experts' hope for a possible fusion of Pakistan and Afghanistan. That would have secured Pakistan from a possible threat from across the Hindu Kush (Soviet Union). If it could be possible, it was seen as the powerful eastern bastion for the Islamic world.[31] It is a far cry from what some Pakistani security experts now

[28]Kenneth Cragg; *Counsels in Contemporary Islam*; pp. 22,25,28; in Ibid. p. 229

[29]Mujahid; n. 27. p. 247

[30]CM Naim; (Ed.) *Iqbal, Jinnah and Pakistan; The Vision and Reality;* New York; Syracuse University; South Asia Series; n. 5; 1979; p. 196

[31]Aslam Siddiqui; Pakistan Seeks Security; Longman's Green & Co.; Lahore; 1960; p. 53.

think of a possible unity of Afghanistan and Pakistan as a bastion for a confrontation with India.

Shaukat Ullah Ansari, a Congressman, had pointed out in 1944 that Pakistan would have insufficient resources to defend itself without outside help.[32] It was as early as 1 September 1947 that the then Finance Minister of Pakistan Ghulam Mohammad approached the US *charge d'affaires* with a plea for providing assistance to his country to meet the administrative expenses, including in particular the defense needs of the Government of Pakistan. Later, the Pakistani representative in Washington, Laik Ali, requested for a sum of $2 billion and included a provision for payment of army personnel.[33] Even the geographical oddity of Pakistan consisting of two wings separated from each other by a thousand miles of Indian Territory had not caused any unease among the Pakistani strategists who had blithely claimed that the battle for East Pakistan would be fought in West Pakistan.[34]

A jehadi culture is evolving in Pakistan, the roots of which are entangled in the Afghan civil war in the 1980s, when the United States set up camps in Pakistan to train terrorists to fight Soviet troops in Afghanistan. General Pervez Musharraf in his 14 August 2001 address had banned two sectarian organisations, Lashkare Jhangvi (Sunni) and Sipah-e-Mohammad (Shia) and in the same breath he had issued a warning to Sipah-e-Sahaba and Tehrik-e-Jafaria. Sectarianism is the creation of historical and political processes, often bloody, over the 1500- year history of Islam. The rise of sectarianism is not, therefore, a new phenomenon; two developments have led to the bloody recrudescence of sectarianism in Pakistan, the Iranian revolution and the Soviet intervention in Afghanistan. In Pakistan General Zia-ul-Haq, during his more than

[32]Shaukat Ullah Ansari; *Pakistan; The Problem of India*; Lahore; Minerva Book Shop; 1944; p. 105

[33]MS Venkatramani; *The American Role In Pakistan, 1947-1958*; New Delhi; 1982; p. 15

[34]Siddiqui; n. 31; p. 53

a decade long military rule sought to put down political activity where necessary with brute force by banning political parties; he also paved the way for the emergence of non-political groupings and forces. By trying to impose Islamisation which was based on *Hanafi Fiqh* (jurisprudence) with strong overtones of Deobandi school of thought, he alienated the Shiite population of Pakistan.[35]

An important role in the propagation of jehadi culture in Pakistan has been played by the *madrasas* during the eighties when General Zia-ul Haq supported them to secure the support of the religious parties for his regime. They also provided the recruiting ground for troops during the war against the Soviet Army in Afghanistan. In the early period, these *madrasas* were financed from the *Zakat* funds, but later financial assistance came from the rich Pakistanis from within the country and from the Gulf. Without government supervision, these *madrasas* were free to preach a narrow and violent version of Islam.[36]

Jehadi *madrasas* and terrorist organisations are promoting sectarian violence within Pakistan, because the two movements—jehad against the Indians in Kashmir and jehad against the Shias in Pakistan—are inextricably linked. The movements share *madrasas*, camps, bureaucracies and operatives. These schools encourage their graduates, who often cannot find work because of their lack of practical education, to fulfil their spiritual obligations by fighting against Hindus in Kashmir or against Muslims of other sects in Pakistan. Sectarian terrorists have killed or injured thousands of Pakistanis over the last 10 years, even attempting to murder the then Prime Minister Nawaz Sharif three years ago. Sipah-e-Sahaba (SeS), the Sunni sectarian party, has a "profound influence on all Deobandi *madrasas*", according to Mujeeb-ur-Rehman Inqalabi, one of the party's leaders. Deobandi madrasas provide 'mental training' to a significant fraction of the terrorists in Kashmir. Pakistan's most

[35] *The Friday Times*; Lahore, Pakistan; 18 August 2001
[36] *Ibid*; n. 17; p. 119

wanted sectarian terrorist, Riaz Bazra, spends at least part of his time hiding out at an Afghan camp that trains terrorists for Kashmir, according to Pakistani officials. The sectarian terrorists arrested in connection with the plot to assassinate Sharif had reportedly been trained at a camp at Khost, where the jehadi group Harkat-ul-Ansar, which was later renamed as Harkatul Mujahideen, used to train terrorists for Kashmir. It is common to meet terrorists, who had moved from SeS to join groups fighting in Kashmir, without any apparent ideological or political difficulty. Estimates of the size of the jehadi groups vary widely, but most US, Pakistani and Indian experts believe the figures to be around tens of thousands. Militant organisations, within Pakistan, start training their members under the pretext of Kashmir jehad and then use these young men to kill members of the rival sects.

According to a Shia website the mujahideen are young men who are lured into jehad on the promise of an eternal place in Paradise. These young men who mainly come from poor and uneducated families are given two to four weeks training in using fire arms and guerrilla warfare. Once the training is complete the mujahid is ready to strike and is launched into the Valley to carry out his mission. As long as the jehad remains confined to Kashmir against the Indian Army, there is no negative impact on the Pakistani society. The problem arises when sectarian and religious organizations within Pakistan start training their members under the pretext of Kashmir jehad and then use these young men to kill members of the rival sect. Azam Tariq the head of SeS and Masood Azhar the head of Jaish-e-Mohammad (JeM) are great friends and both are old devotees of Haq Nawaz Jhangvi (the founder of SeS). The authorities will never take action against JeM since its a jehadi organisation and is promoting the foreign policy of Pakistan. And SeS by having close links with JeM is abusing the foreign policy of Pakistan to its full advantage against the Shias.[37]

[37] www.shianews.com; 8 July 2001

The Shias have no help from any of the Jehadi groups as almost all these groups are Sunni and sympathetic to SeS. It is the Pakistan's ISI which is involved in training and arming these mujahideen some of whom are used by organizations like SeS to fight their guerrilla war against the Shias. For reasons known only to the ISI, it has not formed any Shia jehadi groups in Kashmir. Surely there are enough Shias in Pakistan to form at least one Shia jehadi group. The foreign policy of Pakistan has really cornered the Shias who have been left on their own to defend themselves against the atrocities of these so-called mujahideen.[38]

Many Arabs who had earlier come to Afghanistan at the behest of the mujahideen groups to join the jehad against to Soviet army, had stayed behind and later joined the terrorist groups in Kashmir. They have no interest in the outcome of the struggle. There is no obligation to produce a result in a jehad, it is an affair between the believer and God and not between the mujahid and his enemy. Jehad does not operate between a territorialised state, but within the *Umma*. One can perform one's jehad anywhere and within any institutional framework (Arabs fighting in Afghanistan and in Jammu and Kashmir).[39]

One Pakistani writer on strategic concepts says that the Holy Quran does not interpret war in terms of narrow national interests. Divine as a concept, but human in its evolution, the Quranic philosophy of war consists of both constant and variable factors. The main strength of this philosophy lies in the strength of the constants. He goes on to say that the basis of the study of 'Islamic' concepts of 'strategy' is to understand the difference between total strategy that is 'jehad' and military strategy. The term 'jehad' so often confused with military strategy, is in fact the near equivalent of total or grand strategy. Jehad is a continuous and never ending struggle waged on all fronts including political, economic, social, psychological,

[38] *Ibid.*

[39] Roy; n. 9. p. 66

domestic, moral, and spiritual, to attain the object of policy. He has put forward the idea of a '*Millat* army' or '*Millat* at arms' which will be some kind of a mass army comprising the Muslim community. The idea is that jehad, the Quranic concept of total strategy, demands the preparation and application of total national power and military instruments is one of its elements.[40]

[40]Col. (Retd.) S. G. Mehdi; 'Imperatives for Changing Colonial Defence Concepts,' *Defence Journal*, November 1338

CHAPTER 5

The Taliban-al-Qaida after One Year of War

Sreedhar

On 7 October 2002, the US-led war on terrorism, Operation Enduring Freedom, completed one year. The primary objective of this war was to completely destroy the Taliban-al-Qaida network in Afghanistan. It is an unusual war in many ways. Up to August 1998, the Taliban-al-Qaida were friends of the US and were used by the US to achieve strategic objectives in South and Southwest Asia. After the August 1998 attacks in Dar-e-Salam and Nairobi, they suddenly became wanted persons; and after 11 September 2001, they became adversaries. There are no ground forces of the enemy for the US and its allies to do carpet bombing on like they did at the time of Operation Desert Storm in 1991. The adversary for the US is 'invisible'. The enemy for the US is continuously on the move, making it that much more difficult for the US to attack. This is a peculiar war, which the US is fighting for the first time.

Even now one is not clear what happened to the Taliban-al-Qaida leadership and thousands of their cadres. Media reports indicate that the theatre of war quietly shifted from Afghanistan to Pakistan as most of the Taliban-al-Qaida cadres shifted to Pakistan. The US is in no position to repeat the war strategy adopted in Afghanistan in Pakistan. Meanwhile, the Taliban-al-Qaida are quickly regrouping and have started guerilla operations against enemy targets. A stalemate appears to have been reached on the battlefront with all indications that it may get prolonged.

These aspects require detailed examination. What is the status of the Taliban-al-Qaida combine after one year of relentless pursuit by the US and its allies and in which direction is the war moving?

There are no definite estimates of the strength of Taliban-al-Qaida forces in Afghanistan. They comprised:

- The real Taliban, that is, young students belonging to both Pakistan and Afghanistan and other nationalities from madrasas in Pakistan.
- Former Afghan mujahideen including Mullah Omar himself and his band of followers.
- Veterans of the anti-Soviet campaign who do not belong to any group nor are committed to any ideology, but are individuals who found the opportunity to exercise their vocation of fighting in the fold of the Taliban.
- Previous members of the Khalq faction of the Communist Party of Afghanistan—most of them Soviet-trained professional soldiers.
- Serving and former personnel of the Pakistani armed forces.
- Members of the dissident movements in the Islamic world who are supposed to be assisting the Taliban leadership.

According to a Russian diplomat and academic, the Taliban-al-Qaida leadership has three broad features, as happens with any religion-driven militant movement. At the top are the spiritual heads - Mullah Omar and Osama bin Laden; they have a chain of officials, clergy and military commanders who are controllable. This has been the case in Lebanon, Iran and other places. Under them are commanders, mostly mercenaries, who cannot survive without fighting. The third faction comprises educated people who form layers of administration, including diplomats and governors. Their number is small and they do not count for much, as they lack political or military clout.[1]

[1]For strenght of the Taliban-al-Qaida see Sreedhar and Mahendra Ved *The Afghan Buzkashi-Power Games and Gamesmen* (New Delhi: Wordsmiths 2000).

After the formation of the International Islamic Front for Jehad Against the US and Israel in February 1998, the membership of the Taliban-al-Qaida is reported to have increased to over 200,000. In fact, various accounts originating from the US estimate that they are spread over 70 countries. No one still has a clear picture of how many their sympathizers are, how many are their supporters and how many the active cadres of the Taliban-al-Qaida. Prior to 11 September 2001, it was estimated by various Indian agencies that the Taliban-al-Qaida active cadres in Afghanistan-Pakistan area were in the region of about 55,000 including 15,000 Pakistani military personnel.[2]

When the US and its allies started aerial bombing on 7 October 2001, the Taliban-al-Qaida's strategy was to retreat quickly as they were not militarily prepared to fight an air-land battle. Initially this retreat was seen from two angles. At one level, the observers saw it as a tactical retreat since the Taliban-al-Qaida had no effective answer to the enormous technical superiority of the US war machine. The Taliban-al-Qaida regrouped and offered resistance as the US forces advanced from the north to the south of Afghanistan. At another level, some observers felt that the Taliban-al-Qaida were on the run as their chief patron, Pakistan, made a U-turn in its policy towards them.[3]

As the US and allied forces started advancing, a systematic shifting of the Taliban-al-Qaida bases into Pakistan was seen. Now one can say with a certain amount of definitiveness, that this shift of the Taliban-al-Qaida leadership to Pakistan is for four main reasons:

- There is a long land border, which can be crossed over very easily without being noticed by any surveillance authority. In act, the Taliban-al-Qaida combine's crossing into Pakistan started sometime in late October 2001; at that time, surveillance of the

[2]Estimates made by various Indian Intelligence Agencies.

[3]See various statements made by Gen Pervez Musharraf during September 2001. He even argued that the shift he is making is good for Pakistan's national interest.

Pakistan-Afghanistan border by the US and its allies was not intense enough to detect those crossing over.

- A section of the government in Pakistan is friendly and loyal to the Taliban-al-Qaida leadership and can provide safe havens without much difficulty.
- In the existing anarchic situation in Pakistan, it is easy for an organization like the Taliban-al-Qaida combine to relocate their bases.
- The US and it allies cannot do carpet bombing in Pakistan. Therefore, they have to virtually do a door-to-door search to track down the 50,000 odd Taliban-al-Qaida leadership and cadres. It appears to be quite clear that it is not going to be an easy task for the US to search for them among the 140 million Pakistani populations.

In fact, if one watches the US military operations from mid-December 2001 onwards, the focus of the war gradually shifted from Afghanistan to Pakistan.

Once the war shifted to Pakistan, the US and its allies were forced to take the help of locals extensively. There are also unconfirmed reports that, like they did in the 1980s, the US forces are now taking help from the drug barons in Pakistan and Afghanistan to track the movement of the Taliban-al-Qaida leadership and cadres. There are reports that by March 2002, the US had taken over the management of the Pakistan security apparatus the Inter Service Intelligence Agency (ISI) including the armed forces.[4] Inspire of all these measures, success so far is extremely limited.

This limited success is for two reasons. As a first principle of Jehad (holy war) the Taliban-al-Qaida cadres penetrated the Pakistani armed forces over the years and they did succeed in their efforts. The

[4]According to one diplomat, it is the US Federal Bureau of Investigation that is running the security apparatus at top level in Pakistan (Interview with Arab diplomat on 14 May 2002). Also see the *New York Times*, 14 July 2002. According to the *NYT*, the US FBI is working in close cooperation with Pakistani law enforcement agencies.

lower rank and file in the Pakistani armed forces are disillusioned at the way the top leadership is providing direction to the country. They perceive that an Islamic form of government, like the Taliban in Afghanistan, is the only solution to take Pakistan forward. The Taliban-al-Qaida leadership also perceived that the US and its allies would not be able to disarm the entire Pakistani Army and replace it with their men. Secondly, the Taliban-al-Qaida leadership was also able to evoke the traditional tribal loyalties across the border provinces in Pakistan, in NWFP and Balochistan. The time tested tribal loyalties are more effective than the directives from Islamabad. One saw reports in the Pakistani press that the administration has no control over Federally Administered Tribal Areas like Waziristan. Therefore, if the field level operatives of the Pakistani armed forces are won over by co-opting them into the Taliban-al-Qaida way of thinking, shifting their base to Pakistan for the time being, is quite safe.

In this extraordinary situation, suddenly the war in Afghanistan appears to have reached a 'no win' situation for either side. The Taliban-al-Qaida leadership along with their cadres are sitting quietly, forcing the adversary to take the initiative.

The next question that arises is, what is going to happen to this Taliban-al-Qaida leadership and its cadres?

In the first three months of the US operations, though no clear picture emerged, the number of casualties suffered by the Taliban-al-Qaida is roughly estimated to be in the region of 5,000 cadres killed or wounded and a more or less equal number taken as prisoners of war. Along with this there were a number of civilians too, estimated to be around 30,000. By end June 2002, it was getting increasingly clear that the US has difficulty in identifying who is the Taliban-al-Qaida fighter and who is an ordinary citizen in Afghanistan and Pakistan. Therefore, at the end of one year of US-led military operations the Taliban-al-Qaida network is crippled to a certain extent but not finished. The top leadership remains intact and only some cadres are lost.

INDICATIONS OF REGROUPING

Since the beginning of 2002, the Taliban-al-Qaida, by a series of actions, demonstrated that they are a still a potent force. These include:

- Killing of Daniel Pearl, a journalist of Jewish-Christian origin working with *Wall Street Journal* in Karachi.
- Killing of 11 French engineers, working in Pakistan on a submarine project in Karachi
- Blowing up of a church in Islamabad where some US diplomats were offering their Sunday prayers.
- Bomb blast near the US Consulate in Karachi.
- A plot hatched to pump poisonous gas fumes into the US Embassy in Italy.
- Suspected culprit for making dirty bombs being arrested in the US.
- Assassination of two ministers in the interim government of Hamid Karzai in Kabul in broad daylight.

Except in the Daniel Pearl murder case, in all the others, in Pakistan and Afghanistan, the culprits are yet to be traced by authorities concerned.

In addition to these random attacks on Western targets, the Taliban-al-Qaida cadres are also offering resistance to the US forces in the mountainous region in southern Afghanistan. The early March 2002 surprise attack on a US helicopter, killing six American soldiers, is one incident, which has been reported extensively in the media. The people visiting Kabul and its surrounding areas also mentioned similar stray incidents.

At another level, new arms and ammunition are coming to the Taliban-al-Qaida fighters. In fact, the US Defence Secretary in an interview to the *Washington Times* disclosed that in Afghanistan "We have recently (May-June 2002) discovered some new stuff that is not old and it is modern. It is expensive, it is well done", he said without disclosing where the equipment was found. He said it included "25 backpacks all well done with the right equipment and modern stuff and professionally done."[5]

In another interview to CNN, he observed that he was amazed at the quantity of weapons that have been accumulated in Afghanistan throughout its long history of warfare. "Literally you cannot imagine the hundreds of things, armoured vehicles and rockets, everything under the sun. Surface-to-air missiles. It must be from 20 different countries," he said. In his assessment the Taliban-al-Qaida forces remained probably in one-third of 32 provinces in Afghanistan.[6]

GROUND REALITIES

The Taliban-al-Qaida rule was over in Afghanistan by November 2001, when Kabul was taken over by the US assisted anti-Taliban forces. The US and Afghan forces are hounding their leaders and cadres round the clock but, there are still a considerable number of hard core Taliban in the Southern provinces with large quantities of arms and ammunition including Stinger missiles that may pose a threat to new rulers in Kabul.[7]

The US forces stationed at Kandahar and the new Afghan administration in these provinces is well aware of their presence. The US through the Karzai government is continuing its efforts to win over the tribal elders who were staunch supporters of the Taliban during their six-year rule.[8]

According to a conservative assessment by the government in January 2002, there are over 10,000 Taliban fighters in the provinces

[5]Report in *The News* (Karachi), 29 June 2002. References to Pakistani media were taken from *POT* (Pakistan series), New Delhi.

[6]*Ibid*

[7]I have drawn freely from a *Newsline* story about this aspect. This aspect seems to have not been touched in this fashion by the western media. *Newsline*, February 2002.

[8]*Ibid.*

of Kandahar, Urzugan, Zabul, Helmand, Ghazni and Nimroz and in some parts of Farah and Herat who can rise in revolt when a call comes from their leaders. The number of Taliban supporters is estimated at many times more than their fighters.[9]

The Pakistani media reports say that some Taliban have simply switched their allegiance from Mullah Omar to Mullah Naqib's nominee, Corps Commander Khan Mohammed. Mullah Naqib, a Corps Commander during the days of the mujahideen government, extended his full support to the Taliban when they rose to power and developed a close relationship with Mullah Omar.[10]

Mullah Naqib is the man who brokered the deal between Hamid Karzai and Omar before the latter disappeared from Kandahar with hundreds of his men. However, Mullah Naqib was handed over control of Kandahar along with over 3,000 Taliban fighters, hundreds of vehicles and all the military hardware of the cantonment.[11]

The Governor of Kandahar, Mohammad Shafiq Sherzai, alias Gul Agha, whose forces succeeded in capturing towns and strategic points from Takht Pul to Kandahar airport in the wake of intense US bombing, was critical of this deal and opposed the handing over of Kandahar to his onetime arch-rival, Mullah Naqib. There was also a severe clash between Mullah Naqib and Sherzai's men when the former forcibly entered the city and captured the governor's house. Later, Hamid Karzai, as leader of the interim government, brought about reconciliation between the two. Under the settlement, Sherzai was accepted as Governor while the office of Corps Commander, the number two slot, was given to Mullah Naqibullah who nominated his brother-in-law, Khan Mohammad, to the post. Since then there has been tension between the Governor and his second-in-command. Both men are uneducated, but Sherzai communicates with the

[9] *Ibid.*
[10] *Ibid.*
[11] *Ibid.*

Americans through his two English-speaking cousins, Engineer Yousaf Pashtun and Khaid Pashtun. The Kandahar region is now in the process of building an army of over 20,000 men that may include a sizeable number of Taliban, although the government's edict enforcing the trimming of beards may keep some of them out.[12]

There are reports that in Ghazni alone, north of Kandahar, there are hundreds of vehicles and tanks, besides hundreds of Taliban leaders and fighters under the protection of tribal elders. An equal number are present in the Baghran Mountains to the north in Helmand province where American and Afghan forces tried in vain to track down Mullah Omar and his men.[13]

In Ghazni, the government is reported to be in close contact with tribal leaders to persuade them to surrender the Taliban leaders along with tanks and vehicles. In return, the elders have demanded financial benefits for themselves and amnesty for the Taliban leaders.[14]

In January 2002, Rais Abdul Wahid, a powerful warlord in Baghran, a Tora Bora-like mountainous area, agreed to cooperate in the search in the wake of threats by US forces to bombard the area. The search met with no success and some people believe Rais may have delayed it to give Mullah Omar enough time to get away.[15]

Many Taliban have now resumed their religious studies in Afghanistan and Pakistan or resumed their duties as peshimams or muezzins in the mosques in both countries. Some have gone back to their villages and are biding their time. Some of them roam the streets of Kandahar in the same dress and turban while some have changed their garb.[16]

"The Taliban exist everywhere. They cannot be separated from Pashtun culture. It is not necessary that they rise under the same

[12]*Ibid.*
[13]*Ibid.*
[14]*Ibid.*
[15]*Ibid.*
[16]*Ibid.*

name, but they could launch another movement on the same lines," said Talib Qari Noorduddin, who recently got the job of peshimam in the city of Kandahar. Hundreds of people, many of whom were Taliban, protested in front of the governor's house against the government's decision to cut off food and water to the Arab fighters entrenched in Mir Wais hospital in January-February 2002.[17]

When Governor Gul Agha invited citizen's suggestions regarding the government's day-to-day affairs, very few people showed up. Later, in order to mobilize public opinion for holding a Loya Jirga, the government arranged public meetings and repeatedly requested the people to attend them, but its pleas went unheeded, as not more than 5,000 people in one meeting, 3,000 of whom were primary school children, showed up. Khalid Pushtun, chief adviser to Governor Sherzai had claimed a day earlier that he expected at least 20,000 people to attend the meeting and demonstrate their support for government policies and the current political process.[18]

In Kandahar many believe that the law and order established by the Taliban will be difficult for the warlords to dismantle, even with US support, and that is one reason why public support is not forthcoming.

There are clear differences between two local forces, one loyal to Governor Sherzai and the other to Corps Commander Khan Mohammad in Kandahar. Khan Mohammad's men were deployed at the Mir Wais hospital, guarding the armed Arab fighters who had demanded safe passage. When the Americans decided to conduct a commando operation against the Arabs, they asked these soldiers to leave and then used Governor Sherzai's forces to launch an attack against the Arabs. This type of visible tussle between warlords is hindering the US efforts to win over tribal leaders with all means at its command.[19]

[17] *Ibid.*
[18] *Ibid.*
[19] *Ibid.*

Haji Bashar Noorzai is one of the leaders who surrendered along with Taliban vehicles and around 1,200 weapons of all types in return for assurance of amnesty. Noorzai hosted a lunch for Governor Sherzai and a senior US military official at Maywant, 40 kilometers west of Kandahar city. Bashar, one of the biggest opium tycoons of Afghanistan, was one of the two tribal leaders of the province of Mullah Omar before his departure. Americans are said to have rewarded Bashar in cash for changing sides and expect him to help in the hunt for Osama, Mullah Omar and other Taliban leaders. Another important tribal warlord, Mullah Salam Rocketti in Zabul surrendered on the same conditions. Pir Ismail Gillani, a spiritual leader in Kandahar, played the main role in brokering this deal.[20]

There are visible differences between the Kandahar and Kabul governments, as the former criticize Hamid Karzai for not exerting effective control over the province. Herat Governor Tooran Ismail has been accused of receiving arms and ammunition from neighbouring Iran and developing friendly relations with its government without the consent of Kabul.[21]

Hamid Karzai, too, lacks clout and influence among the tribal elders. He has yet to consolidate his position. He has also been accused of trying to clear the path to power for his brothers and uncles in the upcoming setup in Kandahar by exploiting his close relationship with ex-monarch Zahir Shah.[22]

SYMPATHY FOR THE TALIBAN-AL-QAIDA

All this indicates three distinct trends in the future of the Taliban-al-Qaida. First, till the time of writing, the Taliban-al-Qaida leadership and cadres were hiding some where under someone's patronage. Whether state actors are providing such patronage or non-state actors

[20] *Ibid.*
[21] *Ibid.*
[22] *Ibid.*

or a combination of the two is now known. The developments since 11 September 2001, especially in terms of attacks on US property and personnel and its allies leads one to assume that it is a combination of the two.

This also brings to the forefront the question as to what is the rationale for state actors to continue to provide patronage to the Taliban-al-Qaida. One can give a number of interpretations for this phenomenon. The Taliban-al-Qaida are the first to challenge the West's hegemony. Their attacks on 11 September projected them in the Islamic world, as a group of people who can challenge the US hegemony. These people appear to have no shortage of sympathizers and money suppliers across the entire Islamic world. They came to Pakistan along with their families without any difficulty in October-November 2001. This clearly indicates, that official policies against them by the Government of Pakistan cannot be implemented effectively. This can be due to the sympathy of lower rungs of the bureaucracy for the Taliban-al-Qaida. It can also be due to the dual policy being followed by the ruling elite in Islamabad. Some even suspect that there is a split in the higher echelons of the Pakistani decision-making process. Whatever may be the reason? The Pakistani media is full of accounts of how the officials advised tribal warlords to move away the Taliban-al-Qaida men under their protection to far off places to avoid the US carpet-bombing. These officials never asked the tribal warlords to hand over the Taliban-al-Qaida men to them.

Similarly, the sympathizers of the Taliban-al-Qaida in countries like Saudi Arabia and the UAE feel that they are upholding their "faith" by supporting the Taliban-al-Qaida combine. It was argued extensively by intelligentsia in the Islamic world that Israeli occupation of Palestinian land is the primary reason for this sense of injustice among the Muslims. Since the enemy is more powerful, they argue, the aggrieved can adopt any means to achieve their objective. They also feel that it is their moral duty to support people who are fighting for the cause of their faith. Their logic is also quite persuasive. Those men, when fighting the Red Army from 1979 to 1989, were declared as friends by the US; at that point of time whatever they did was justified in the name of a justifiable cause. The same men while fighting for their own cause suddenly became 'terrorists'.

All this leads one to conclude that whatever measures are adopted by the great powers to eliminate the Taliban-al-Qaida, the latter cannot be eliminated totally. They can at best be silenced temporarily.

PROSPECTS OF GUERILLA WAR

This regrouping and sympathy led to guerilla attacks by the Taliban-al-Qaida combine. According to one Pakistani commentator the rocket attack on US-occupied Khost airbase on the night of 3 March 2002 is an incident in which the Americans were targeted. The US military authorities are claiming that the two rockets failed to cause any human or material damage at the airbase. The US warplanes retaliated by bombing suspected rocket-launcher sites near Khost town.[23]

Later reports indicate that the US had lost one of its soldiers in Khost earlier when a teenager reportedly ambushed a convoy. Another American soldier was wounded in the attack. Media reports indicate that up to end March 2002, Khost and the adjoining Paktia and Paktika provinces remained hostile territory for the Americans even though some tribal commanders are now fighting on the side of the US.[24]

The US-held Kandahar airport came under repeated attacks by unidentified gunmen. The airport, which serves as the biggest US

[23]Rahimullah Yusufzai first commented upon the trends of a guerilla war. I took extensive extracts from his article, "Rahimullah Yusufzai, Guerilla War Began in Afghanistan" in *The News*, 8 March 2002.

[24]*Ibid.*

base in Afghanistan, has been attacked quite a few times since November 2001 despite its extraordinary security. The airport, which also houses contingents of Australian, Canadian and German troops is likely to remain a primary target for remnants of the Taliban and the al-Qaida.[25]

A convoy of US troops was also fired at near Jalalabad during the Tora Bora campaign late last year. An American soldier was injured in the attacks. The killing of a CIA official, Johnny Spann, during the Taliban prisoners' uprising in the Qala Jhangi fort in Mazar Sharif was the first reported American casualty in combat in Afghanistan. It was followed by more American deaths in plane crashes in Afghanistan and Pakistan.[26]

The downing of the MH-47 helicopter by the Taliban and al-Qaida fighters in the combat area near Gardez, capital of Paktia province neighbouring Khost, on 3 March 2002 and the death of six US soldiers in the incident is another indication that the Americans would continue to suffer casualties while serving in a dangerous place like Afghanistan. It would certainly embolden all those who want the US and its allies to pull out their troops from Afghanistan. The more the Americans stay in Afghanistan, the more they would become embroiled in local disputes and expose themselves to retaliation.[27]

Taliban supreme leader, Mohammad Omar, was not taken seriously when he vowed to wage a guerilla war against the US military in Afghanistan. As has been mentioned earlier his Taliban fighters failed to put up much resistance in the face of the intense US aerial strikes and most of them made a hasty retreat from town after town. Unlike the Taliban, Osama bin Laden's al-Qaida fighters fought until death in Tora Bora, Kandahar airport and a few other places. About a dozen injured al-Qaida fighters admitted to the Mirwais hospital in Kandahar before the fall of the city to anti-

[25] *Ibid.*
[26] *Ibid.*
[27] *Ibid.*

Taliban forces also preferred death over surrender and died fighting the US soldiers and their Afghan proxies.[28]

The appearance of the so-called "*shabnamas*" (night-letters) in Afghan cities such as Kandahar, Jalalabad and Khost in early 2002 is another cause for alarm for the US and its allied forces. The pamphlets, mostly in Pashto and some in Persian Dari, declare "jehad" against the foreign troops in Afghanistan as mandatory and urge the Afghans to evict the "occupation forces" from the homeland. They also warn those Afghans cooperating with the USA of serious consequences.[29]

The International Security Assistance Force (ISAF), after enjoying a degree of support in Kabul, is also attracting some criticism. By their own admission, the British troops in the ISAF have been fired at thrice in Kabul. They have suffered no casualties until now, but it seems the British troops are the primary targets for those opposed to the presence of foreign troops in Afghanistan. One reason behind the attacks could be historical because Afghans are very mindful of their history. The British and Afghans fought their wars in the past when the former tried to colonise Afghanistan. The Afghans put up a stiff resistance and won their independence. The return of British troops to Afghanistan is not a very welcome move for some Afghans conscious of their past. Besides, the British troops are seen by many Afghans as America's stronger allies and are thus blamed for the ongoing military campaigns in Afghanistan. The British troops also earned the enmity of many in Kabul when they killed a man who was trying to take his pregnant sister-in-law to hospital in Kabul at night.[30]

LIMITATIONS OF THE US AND ITS ALLIES

In spite of all the support mobilized by the US from its allies and friends across the globe, the sheer logistics of fighting a war in a

[28] *Ibid.*
[29] *Ibid.*
[30] *Ibid.*

country, which is 20,000 miles away, is not an easy task. It is going to be a prolonged and time-consuming war. In addition, the sheer identification of the enemy, the Taliban-al-Qaida leadership and cadres, is also not going to be an easy task. As one Taliban sympathizer told me, "every Afghan living in Pakistan cannot be targeted. The carpet bombing has reached its saturation point in terms of eliminating the Taliban-al-Qaida cadres." In addition, if we go by the US literature's portrayal of Osama bin Laden, he is still around in Afghanistan/Pakistan, knowing fully well that his Pakistani sympathizers can play any number of games to keep the US at bay in tracking him down.

Apparently, the Taliban-al-Qaida combine is working on the principle of tiring out the adversary.[31] If the US and its allies get stuck; like in Vietnam, the domestic pressures in those countries will automatically force them to withdraw. As one commentator put it, the US and its allies are going to commit mistakes like they made on 30 June 2002 (many in a marriage party were killed after being mistaken for a Taliban-al-Qaida group), and people are going to protest over it. The situation can be cleverly exploited by people like Osama to turn the tide against the US in Afghanistan and Pakistan.[32]

In this game of patience, it is extremely difficult even for a superpower to sustain itself for a prolonged period across the seven seas.

CONCLUSION

At this point of time the Taliban-al-Qaida combine is down but not out. They surrendered Kabul but not beyond that. There seems to be an element of truth that a low intensity conflict, more in the form of guerrilla warfare, will continue in Afghanistan for quite some time to come. In the process what the US Central Command incharge of operations in Afghanistan can do and cannot do in an

[31]Why bin Laden is so hard to catch, <www.themoscowtimes.com>, / stories/ 2002/04/007 html

[32]*Ibid.*

unconventional war fought by unconventional means, is being clearly exposed. For the time being the Afghans tired of more than two decades of war, may feel comfortable with the US efforts. But the Taliban-al-Qaida has been allowed to escape and regroup itself in Pakistan and the US is now completely dependent on Pakistan to achieve its war objectives; now much depends on Pakistan.

From the Indian perspective, the US war on terrorism has reached a dead end. Some feel it may continue for years and the US may slow down the tempo of operations. The cumbersome ground operations in Pakistan are a time-consuming process with a fair amount of uncertainties. If by any chance the Taliban-al-Qaida leadership is caught, the US may immediately call off the war. In such a situation, the compromises the US is making in fighting this inconvenient war would leave some legacies like it did at the time of the 1979-89 US war against the Soviet Union in Afghanistan; drug money being one example. That means India has to prepare itself to fight its war against terrorism, which has become transnational in character. The convergence of Indian and US interests is, therefore, accidental and limited to fighting terrorism.

CHAPTER 6

Al-Qaeda's Asian Network

Rohan Gunaratna

With the dramatic changes in the international political environment at the end of the East-West confrontation, the face of terrorism has transformed. Unlike the Cold War terrorist groups, post-Cold War terrorist groups pose a much higher threat to both governments and society. While the terrorist groups of the 1970s killed in tens, the groups in the 1980s and 1990s killed in 100s. With the dawn of the 21st century, terrorist intentions were clearly spelled out by Osama bin Laden, on 12 November 2002:

"When will fear, killing, destruction, expulsion, orphaning and widowing remain only limited to us while security, stability and happiness remains only limited to you? This is an unfair allotment. The time has come to share in these matters equally. Just like you kill, you will be killed. And just like you bombarded, you will be bombarded. Be prepared to receive the glad tidings of what will be bad for you. By the grace of Allah, the Islamic Ummah (nation) has started to fire at you with its sincere youth, who have promised Allah to continue Jihad with words and swords, in order to defend the truth and to extinguish the falsehood till the last drop of blood."[1]

AL-QAEDA—THE REAL THREAT

Al-Qaeda Al Sulbah (The Solid Base) is the first multinational terrorist group of the 21st century. While past and present terrorist

[1]Osama bin Laden, Al-Jazeera Satellite television, Qatar 12 November 2002.

groups generally have a national base, limiting their terrorist campaigns to a single theatre, al-Qaeda is an umbrella organization waging multiple campaigns, both against the West and Muslim regimes friendly to the West. In addition to its core force of 3,000 members, al-Qaeda has established linkages with two-dozen Islamist groups. Driven by the ideal of a universal Jihad, al-Qaeda has been able to politicize, radicalize and mobilize Muslims both in the territorial communities of the Middle East and Asia as well as in the migrant communities of Europe, North America, and Australia. As a group with global reach, al-Qaeda presents a new kind of threat, hitherto unimagined by counter-terrorism practitioners and security and intelligence professionals alike.

Between pre-modern Afghanistan and post-modern continental United States via Europe and Asia, al-Qaeda has built a state-of-the-art terrorist network for moving funds, goods and personnel to attack its targets.[2] It is the painstaking and steadfast construction of this network over many years that enabled al-Qaeda to mount 9/11. Al-Qaeda targeting reflects its sophistication as a professional terrorist group. After the East Africa bombing—a land suicide attack on a diplomatic target—the US security community strengthened the security of all US missions overseas. However, instead of another land suicide operation, al-Qaeda mounted a sea-borne suicide operation. After al-Qaeda attacked USS Cole in October 2000, the US security community invested in preventing another land or maritime attack by strengthening perimeter security. However, al-Qaeda evaded the security measures and struck America's most outstanding landmarks from the sky. Thereafter, al-Qaeda planned to strike the US once more with a radiological dispersal device using Jose Perdilla, an American Muslim; an operation that was disrupted at the reconnaissance stage. In keeping with al-Qaeda's 'losing and learning doctrine', it is likely to attempt to destroy the third target,

[2]Al-Qaeda is able to build a state-of-the-art global network because it is a diverse group it has recruited worldwide.

the US Congress in the future.[3] As terrorist groups copy cost effective tactics, al-Qaeda is likely to use civilian infrastructure once again to attack Western targets.

In keeping with its founding charter authored by its founder Sheikh Dr Abdullah Azzam in March 1988, al-Qaeda is the "spearhead of Islam" or "the pioneering vanguard of the Islamic movements".[4] Because of the inspirational value, al-Qaeda's preference is to attack strategic targets usually resorting to suicide attacks (martyrdom operations). Attacking high prestige and symbolic strategic targets generally requires extensive planning and preparation over a long period of time across several countries. Al-Qaeda expects the Muslims it instigates and the Islamic movements it inspires to strike at least tactical targets. To strengthen Islamic movements worldwide al-Qaeda together with its erstwhile host—the Islamic Movement of Taliban, the de-facto government of the Islamic Emirate of Afghanistan and its previous incarnation, the Maktab al Khidamat lil Mujahideen al Arab—trained several tens of thousands of Western, Middle Eastern, African, Caucasian, Balkan and Asian Muslims.

DECENTRALIZATION

Al-Qaeda training infrastructure has suffered gravely as a result of US intervention in Afghanistan since October 2001. However, al-Qaeda began decentralizing the organization opening new facilities for training its recruits in many of the regional theatres from Mindanao in the Philippines to Pankishi Valley in Georgia, much before 9/11. In forming the World Islamic Front for Jihad Against the Jews and the Crusaders in 1998, al-Qaeda networked with—and in some cases co-opted—for instance, the Moro Islamic Liberation Front in Southeast Asia to the Islamic Movement of Uzbekistan in Central

[3]As al-Qaeda is a learning organization, al-Qaeda studies all operations where it has suffered losses and improves the next time. Losing and learning doctrine is typical of sophisticated groups.

[4]Abdullah Azzam, al Qaidah al Sulbah, Al Jihad, 41, April 1988, p. 46.

Asia and the Salafist Group for Call and Combat in North Africa. The loss of Afghanistan is a massive blow to al-Qaeda's capability, however, both the support it enjoys in the tribal areas as well as the pre-9/11 decentralization is likely to ensure its survival. With focused targeting on the Afghan-Pakistan border where both al-Qaeda and Taliban (Mullah Omar Faction) are concentrated, the group will depend on its regional networks to continue the fight. Al-Qaeda's Southeast Asian network is an integral part of al-Qaeda. Al-Qaeda's disrupted Singapore operation clearly demonstrates the group's intentions and the capabilities as well as the opportunities for attack in target rich Far East. Therefore, the threshold for terrorism—both support for conducting attacks and the attacks themselves—has clearly increased in Southeast Asia.

Al-Qaeda has adapted to the dismantlement of its training infrastructure in Afghanistan. Although al-Qaeda has neither physically nor ideologically abandoned Afghanistan, it is seeking to compensate for the loss of a state-of-the-art training infrastructure and operational base by continuing to work together with the local groups. As much as the local groups have depended on al-Qaeda in the past, the parent organisation has depended on the local groups. Immediately after al-Qaeda bombed the US diplomatic targets in East Africa in August 1998 and Pakistan began to arrest key al-Qaeda operatives using its soil for transit into landlocked Afghanistan, Osama bin Laden looked to the Philippines. Peshawar based al-Qaeda's head of foreign operations Zein Al Abideen alias Abu Zubaidah phoned the Moro Islamic Liberation Front (MILF) leadership and requested them to open new training facilities for foreign recruits in February 1999. Until the Camp Abu Bakr complex was overrun, al-Qaeda recruits from Malaysia, Singapore and Indonesia trained in its satellite camps Hodeibia, Palestine and Vietnam. Thereafter, the training facility moved to Poso in Sulawesi and after its closure, to Balikpapan in Kalimanthan, where al-Qaeda continued to train its Southeast Asian and other recruits until 9/11.

Al-Qaeda's post-9/11 pronouncements—including Abu Gaith Sulayman's recorded message—reflect both its intention and will to attack Western, especially US targets, Although al-Qaeda has lost its key leaders such as its military commander Mohommad Atef alias Abu Hafs, al-Qaeda's core and penultimate leadership and provides the strategic and tactical direction is still intact.[5] As long as the leadership of a group survives, the group itself will survive. Furthermore, the Islamist milieu, both in the Muslim territorial and migrant communities continue to provide the bulk of the recruits, finance and other forms of support. As the focus of the coalition is largely military, the robust Islamist ideology of al-Qaeda—that has gone unchallenged—is ensuring the survival of the group. Al-Qaeda is replenishing its human losses (killed, captured, and arrested) and material wastage (weapons and other supplies) both inside and outside Afghanistan. As a result, al-Qaeda's global network—with members drawn from 46 countries and activities in 98 countries—is still functional, including its operatives in Europe.[6] Although al-Qaeda operational cells planning and preparing for attacks have been disrupted in France, The Netherlands, Belgium, Germany, Italy, Spain and the UK, al-Qaeda support cells disseminating propaganda, raising funds, recruiting, procuring supplies, and mounting surveillance on intended targets are still active. Its collaborators, supporters and sympathisers are filling the leadership vacuum created by the first wave of arrests of al-Qaeda leaders in Europe immediately after 9/11. The post-9/11 al-Qaeda cells are more clandestine, compact and self-contained, thus hard to detect and disrupt. As such, Western societies and their governments will face a long-term continuous threat from al-Qaeda.

THE EVOLVING THREAT

Post-9/11 al-Qaeda attempted but failed to destroy US, UK, Australian and Israeli diplomatic missions and attack a US warship

[5]Rohan Gunaratna, *Inside al-Qaeda: Global Network of Terror* (New York: Columbia University Press, 2002), p. 227-9.

[6]CIA estimate.

off Singapore; US and British warships in the Straits of Gibraltar; and poison the water supply to the US embassy in Rome. In addition to Richard Reid, the shoe bomber trying to destroy an aircraft over the Atlantic, al-Qaeda also attempted to bomb the US embassy and American cultural centre in Paris and attack the US base in Sarajevo. An al-Qaeda Sudanese member fired a surface-to-air missile at a US warplane taking off from the Prince Sultan airbase in Saudi Arabia in December 2001. Al-Qaeda suicide bombers also attacked a French oil tanker off Yemen and US troops in Kuwait in October 2002. To instigate Islamists to strike worldwide Jewish targets, Nizar Seif Eddin al-Tunisi (meaning Sword of the Faith, the Tunisian) alias Nizar Nouar, an al-Qaeda Tunisian suicide bomber in a Liquid Petroleum Gas vehicle rammed Ghriba Synagogue, Africa's oldest Jewish synagogue, killing 14 German tourists, including one child, and 5 Tunisians in Djerba, Tunisia on 11 April 2002.[7]

Due to the difficulty of operating in the post-9/11 environment, al-Qaeda has delegated and diffused many of its responsibilities to other Islamist movements (parties and groups) that operated under the al-Qaeda umbrella. In a number of theatres, al-Qaeda is operating through several groups with whom it hitherto shared training, financial and operational infrastructure in Afghanistan. This phenomenon is most visible in Pakistan where two-dozen attacks by al-Qaeda and its associated groups have occurred until today. Beginning with the massacre of the Christians in Bhawalpur in the Punjab district in October 2001, al-Qaeda has launched a number of terrorist operations including the kidnapping and murder of the *Wall Street journal* journalist Daniel Pearl and a church bombing in Islamabad killing a US diplomat's wife and daughter. A suicide bomber of Harakat-ul Mujahidin-al-Aalami, an al-Qaeda associate group killed 11 Frenchmen and 12 Pakistanis on 18 May 2002. The well-planned attack was conducted after mounting

[7]Al-Qaeda's front The Islamic Army for the Liberation of the Holy Sites claimed the attack and subsequently an interview by Abdel Azeem Al Muhajir, an al-Qaeda military commander, confirmed it as an al-Qaeda operation.

surveillance on the Sheraton hotel and the bus route used by French naval engineers and technicians working on the submarine project in Karachi. The suicide vehicle bomb attack by an al-Qaeda associate group against the US Consulate in Karachi on 14 June 2002 injured a US marine and killed 11 Pakistanis. Using the same vehicle, they also targeted President Musharraf on 26 April 2002, but the remote control failed to detonate the explosives-laden vehicle.

While the Taliban is a guerrilla force, al-Qaeda remains a terrorist group. The Taliban operates somewhat openly and al-Qaeda operates clandestinely. The Taliban-al-Qaeda combined strategy is to install a regime that is friendly to the Islamists in Pakistan. If not, they are aiming to install at least a regime neutral to the Islamists. They believe that the future survival of al-Qaeda and Taliban along the Afghanistan-Pakistan border will depend on their ability to generate sustained support from Pakistan. As such, they are likely to target Musharraf repeatedly until he is killed or removed from office. Al-Qaeda also mounted at least two clandestine operations to assassinate President Hamid Karzai or cabinet ministers. After a traffic accident, an Afghan and a foreigner in an explosives (Semtex)-laden Toyota were both arrested in the centre of Kabul on 29 July 2002. In September 2002, al-Qaeda mounted a second assassination operation that was disrupted by Karzai's US bodyguards and immediately after, an unknown group positioned a claymore mine on a route usually taken by the Presidential motorcade.

PRIMARY TARGET

The United States, the 'head of the poisonous snake', remains the principal target of al-Qaeda. Al-Qaeda's preference was reflected when Osama said, 'The battle has moved to inside America. We will continue this battle, God permitting, until victory or until we meet God.'[8] Until the US intelligence agencies infiltrate terrorist groups, a task that cannot be accomplished in the short term (one or two

[8]Interview, al-Jazeera's Kabul correspondent Tayseer Allouni, 21 October 2001.

years), it is reasonable to assume that the US is as vulnerable as it was before 9/11. The governments that assist the US in its campaign in Afghanistan as well as the governments that have disrupted al-Qaeda cells on their soil have earned the wrath of al-Qaeda. After, for example, the Singaporean government disrupted cells of Jamaah Islamiyah (Al-Qaeda's Southeast Asian arm operating in Singapore), the leadership relocated in Indonesia have vowed to crash a plane on to the Changi international airport in Singapore. Similarly, in retaliation for Pakistan's support to the US, several Islamist groups in Pakistan are attacking soft targets nationwide. For instance, Islamist terrorists killed four Pakistanis at a Christian school for children of foreign aid workers in Murree Hills on 5 August and three others in the church of a Christian hospital in Taxila on 9 August 2002. Several other revengeful attacks have occurred. An explosion killed the Mayor and 12 others in Mindanao, Philippines on Christmas Eve of 2002.

The threat picture clearly shows that al-Qaeda is constrained from launching another large-scale attack such as 9/11. However, al-Qaeda is still able to conduct small and medium scale attacks. With unprecedented security, intelligence and law enforcement cooperation as well as with heightened public alertness, al-Qaeda is unable to engage in extensive and long-term planning and preparation across more than one country, a pre-requisite for conducting coordinated simultaneous attacks. Nonetheless, once al-Qaeda patiently identifies the gaping holes in the post-9/11 security architecture, its super cells may be able to plan, prepare and execute mass casualty attacks. For the time being due to the limitations of mounting large-scale operations al-Qaeda is considering a range of options. They range from attacking population centres, economic infrastructure, and symbolic/high prestige targets inside the US. While some of al-Qaeda's super cells are 'going to sleep' or hibernating, others are preparing to take opportunity targets. Of the three dozen large, medium and small-scale attacks conducted by al-Qaeda and its associate groups against US, allied, and coalition targets worldwide only a fraction have been successful. Al-Qaeda has learnt that they have failed due to tighter international, especially US, security countermeasures and hurried al-Qaeda planning. Nonetheless, al-Qaeda ideology ensures that like a revengeful and a retaliatory wounded animal the group is determined to strike back. As a result of a range of countermeasures, the threat is shifting, stretching the threat spectrum to include a wider range of targets as well as a change in the *modus operandi.* Al-Qaeda is operating through other Islamist groups providing them trainers and funds thereby influencing their strategic and tactical direction. Al-Qaeda is likely to operate through associated groups for as long as the threat to it remains.

IMPORTANCE OF AFGHANISTAN-PAKISTAN

The developments in Afghanistan and Pakistan are central to the future survival of the Taliban and al-Qaeda. These two groups are adapting to the security environment and can be seen to have undergone three internal strategic changes. First, Mullah Omar, the leader of the Taliban and the former head of the Islamic Emirate of Afghanistan, has assumed the principal responsibility to fight the US-led coalition forces in Afghanistan. In the fight, Osama bin Laden himself has pledged loyalty and allegiance to his leadership. As Osama went into hiding, as the 'leader of the Faithful', Mullah Omar spearheaded the regrouping and re-organizing of the Taliban after 9/11. After re-establishing communication with the scattered units of the Taliban, he regrouped them along secure areas of the 2446 kilometres long Afghanistan-Pakistan border. As they did during the Soviet period, their dream is to consolidate the strength of the Taliban and deepen their strategic influence in Afghanistan and Pakistan by preparing for a campaign of protracted guerrilla warfare. To rebuild support, the Taliban indoctrinates the Afghan people both directly by disseminating propaganda and through supporters and sympathisers scattered throughout Afghanistan.

Second, over the past year, the Taliban and al-Qaeda have replaced losses in the rank and file by promoting middle level and junior leaders as well as by fresh recruitment. To compensate for the total loss of state support from Pakistan to the Taliban, Mullah Omar has established Lashkar-e-Omar—a covert network of support organizations in Pakistan—to sustain a low intensity campaign in Afghanistan and in the area. By instigating its associate groups in Kashmir such as Harakat-ul Mujahideen and Jaish-e-Mohommad to intensify the violence in Kashmir, the Taliban forced Pakistan to re-deploy its troops on the Afghan border along the 2414 kilometres long India-Pakistan border. With the increase in the porosity of the Pakistan-Afghanistan border, the Taliban and al-Qaeda have re-established their lines of communication, supplies and recruits into Pakistan. The Taliban, al-Qaeda, and other associate groups are all harnessing the Islamist milieu in Pakistan and overseas (both territorial and migrant) to ensure a revival in support (encouragement, funds and supplies) necessary for survival and sustenance. Conflicts of international neglect where Muslims are suffering—Palestine, Kashmir, Chechnya, Maluku, Mindanao and Algeria, among others—ensure continuity of support. Except during the first three months of confrontation, there are no signs of mass desertions from the Taliban or al-Qaeda indicating the state of morale within the rank and file.

Third, al-Qaeda's deputy leader Dr Ayman al-Zawahiri is playing a more substantial role in al-Qaeda support and operational activities both inside and outside Afghanistan. To topple Karzai in Afghanistan and Musharraf in Pakistan, al-Qaeda has established networks of collaborators, supporters and sympathisers in both these countries. To coordinate and conduct operations al-Qaeda is seeking to re-establish communication with its associate groups and command cells respectively. To revive support al-Qaeda is establishing links with its affiliate NGOs and other charities overseas. With the failure of al-Qaeda to strike tactical US, allied, and coalition targets worldwide after 9/11, the group is considering reverting to both tactical and strategic targets. The group is also considering revisiting the maritime and the Chemical, Biological, Radiological and Nuclear (CBRN) scenarios, options al-Qaeda considered over the years. For instance, Osama paid USD 1.5 million to a Sudanese military officer to purchase a Uranium canister from South Africa. Al-Qaeda was duped when the group was sold an externally radiated canister. Although suicide terrorism, coupled with conventional attacks, have proved to be the most effective, al-Qaeda and its associated groups are likely to go down the road of chemical, biological and radiological terrorism.

Al-Qaeda has inspired and instigated a wider constituency of groups and individuals to take on the fight for Allah. As seen in a number of sporadic attacks in Europe, North Africa, Indonesia, Pakistan and Kashmir, Islamist groups are considering a range of options—arson, shooting, throwing grenades, and exploding Improvised Explosive Devices against Jewish, Christian and Hindu targets. The Islamists continue to inspire and instigate violence against 'the enemies of Islam', 'the infidels' and the 'unbelievers' both by word of mouth and in over a 1,000 sites on the worldwide web. The Islamists are operating across a wide spectrum, from for low tech to the high tech, stretching government resources and weakening security countermeasures. This demonstrates the success of al-Qaeda in educating a much wider constituency to challenge the West and Muslim regimes friendly to the West.

SOUTHEAST ASIAN NETWORK

The security and intelligence services, accustomed to collecting intelligence by technical methods, have limited high quality information about the group.[9] Most public officials and academics find it difficult to understand al-Qaeda because the group functions

[9]As al-Qaeda, a secret organization, continues to pose a threat, government intelligence agencies are reluctant to make information about the group public.

both operationally and ideologically. In addition to dispatching its operatives to target countries (such as the 9/11 team led by Mohammed Atta), it provides the experts, training and resources to other Islamist political and military organisations to advance a common goal. Like it has penetrated existing Islamist networks worldwide, al-Qaeda in Southeast Asia penetrated Jemaah Islamiyah (JI), a regional organisation with over ground and underground networks extending from southern Thailand to Australia. Among the groups it has infiltrated and influenced are Kumpulan Mujahideen Malaysia; Jashkar Jundullah, Indonesia; Moro Islamic Liberation Front, Philippines. When JI wanted to destroy the US, British, Australian and Israeli diplomatic targets in Singapore, al-Qaeda dispatched four Afghan-trained Arab suicide bombers to Southeast Asia. In an interview, an al-Qaeda detainee told this author: "We did not want to risk using Asian Muslims for a landmark operation".[10]

By physical and intellectual contact, al-Qaeda members (ideologues, trainers, operatives) and its literature (www.alneda.com) has physically and ideologically strengthened a dozen Islamist terrorist groups, political parties, charities and individuals. In the region, it has created a mission and a vision for the Islamists to create a caliphate comprising Malaysia, Singapore, Brunei, Indonesia, Cambodia and Mindanao. Towards a Darulah Islamiah Raya, about 400 Islamists have been trained in facilities in Afghanistan (Derunta, Khalden, etc.), Pakistan (Karachi, Lahore, Peshawar), Malaysia (Negri Sembilan and other locations), Mindanao in the Philippines (Camp Vietnam, Hodeibia and Palestine in Abu Bakr Complex) and in Indonesia (Poso, Sulawesi and Balikpapan, Kalimanthan) throughout the 1990s. The regional leader Indonesian national Riduan Isamuddin alias Hambali, resident of Malaysia from 1985-1987, who fought in the anti-Soviet multinational Afghan campaign, built the al-Qaeda network in the region from 1991. In addition to

[10]The author interviewed a number of al-Qaeda and Taliban detainees, including the American Taliban John Walker Lindh held in US custody.

its plans to assassinate Pope John Paul II and President Clinton in Manila and explode 11 airliners over the Asia-Pacific in early 1995, al-Qaeda exploded a bomb injuring 11 and killing one Japanese passenger and nearly destroying a Tokyo bound Philippine Airlines flight in December 1994. In addition to bombing the residence of the Philippine Ambassador in Indonesia, al-Qaeda's JI simultaneously bombed 30 churches killing 22 and wounding 96 in Jakarta, West Java, North Sumatra, Riau, Bandung, East Java and Nusatenggara on Christmas eve of 2000 and five targets in Manila on 30 December 2000.[11] It has also played a pivotal role in the violence in Maluku that has killed over 5000 people during the past 5 years. Further, al-Qaeda's Malaysian cell also hosted the USS Cole planners and provided the critical cover, finances (and nearly the flight training) to Zacarias Moussaiou, an arrested 9/11 suicide hijacker. Moussaiou even visited the Malacca Flying Academy in Malaysia to learn to fly. Finally, Moussaiou substituted for Ramzi bin Al Shibh of the Hamburg cell who tried thrice but failed to get a visa to enter the US. Hambali who holds both al-Qaeda and JI membership and featured in all these activities is alive and active. Recent recoveries from Afghanistan examined by the author include documents with extensive references to al-Qaeda's spiritual leader in Southeast Asia Abu Bakar Bashir, Hambali and other directing figures of the al-Qaeda network in the region.

As a result of the Spanish investigation into al-Qaeda, the Indonesian government has reluctantly admitted that al-Qaeda operated a training camp in Poso. "The training camp led by Omar Bandon consisted of 8-10 small villages located side by side on the beach, equipped with light weapons, explosives and a firing range. Participants of the training are not only from the local people but also from overseas. The instructor of the physical training in the camp is Parlindugan Siregar, a member of the al-Qaeda network in

[11]For more details, Rohan Gunaratna, *Inside al-Qaeda: Global Network of Terror* (New York: Columbia University Press, 2002), chapter on al-Qaeda in Asia.

Spain," reported Indonesian intelligence.[12] Both Nic Robertson of CNN in Afghanistan and the Special Branch investigating the al-Qaeda cell in Leicester recovered copies of videotapes of the Poso camp. Except for 10 millennium bombers of the churches, the government has failed to arrest and prosecute both the Poso trainees and the trainers, who are free and active.

THREAT TRAJECTORY

Of all its associate groups, JI has been by far the most active. JI's overt support and covert operational infrastructure is enmeshed with the Muslim socio-economic and political fabric of the Far East. As a closely-knit politico-religious organization, it recruits from families, extended families, neighbourhood, schools, universities, etc. Even before 9/11, JI mounted surveillance on US and Israeli diplomatic targets in the Philippines, US warships in the Straits of Malacca, and multiple targets in Singapore. After 9/11, JI planned the worst terrorist attack in Singapore. After the JI operation to destroy diplomatic targets in Singapore was disrupted in December 2001, governments in the region targeted the JI infrastructure in Malaysia and the Philippines. The only governments that failed to take action were Australia, Thailand and Indonesia. Until the bombing in Bali on 12 October Indonesia denied that terrorists were operating on its soil. Absorbed in blaming Indonesia, governments within and outside the region failed to work steadfastly with President Megawatti and her ministers, officials and the public. While Islamism moved from the periphery to the centre, threatening Indonesia, the neighbourhood and the wider Asia-Pacific region, Australia also did not react.

JI used Australia to disseminate propaganda and raise funds, Thailand to plan, and Indonesia to prepare to strike Bali. The choice of Bali was driven by a number of factors. Due to the arrest of

[12]Al-Qaeda infrastructure in Indonesia, BIN, Jakarta, 2001.

operatives, seizure of assets and countermeasures enacted by Singapore, Malaysia and the Philippines, JI was constrained in mounting an operation in those countries. In Australia, JI cells were almost all support and not combat cells. In Thailand, JI had important functionaries. JI infrastructure was fully operational in Indonesia. As both the structure and perimeter of US and other diplomatic targets were hardened in Jakarta, JI was driven to set its sight on a soft target in Indonesia. Bali was ideal because it was a predominantly Hindu city with 22,000 Australian tourists.

In mid-January 2002, JI operational commander Hambali met with Mohommad Mansour Jabarah, a 21-year-old Canadian operative of al-Qaeda in southern Thailand. Hambali, who trained and fought in Afghanistan from 1987-1991, held dual membership both of the JI and al-Qaeda consultative (shura) councils. Hambali proposed to Jabarah—who was dispatched to the region by Khalid Sheikh Mohommad, head, al-Qaeda's military committee—which he wished to bomb bars, nightclubs and restaurants frequented by Westerners. The decision to strike Bali was made by Hambali in Bangkok. The city was used by two 9/11 hijackers to enter the US in January 2000 and JI operatives, Agus Dwikarna and Fathur Rahman Al Ghozi, now in custody in the Philippines, intended to transit through Bangkok in early 2002.

Based on US debriefing of Jabarah (arrested in Oman and handed over to the Americans) the FBI issued a memo on 22 August 2002, to the regional intelligence community of JI intensions. However, neither the Australian nor the Southeast Asian intelligence agencies succeeded in developing the tactical intelligence to detect and disrupt JI plans to strike Westerners in night clubs, bars and restaurants. After 9/11, al-Qaeda, especially JI, had identified Australia as an enemy but the Australian government never took the threat seriously. Despite the Australian Embassy in Singapore being identified as an al-Qaeda target, Osama bin Laden's statement that Australia had waged a 'crusade' against the Islamic nation and dismembered East Timor, credible intelligence that a number of Afghanistan trained Australians were dispatched on missions to strike targets inside Australia, and Australia's high-profile participation in the campaign in Afghanistan, the Australian government announced a week before Bali that there was no significant threat of terrorism to Australia or to its interests overseas. The lesson of Bali is clear. Countries that tolerate terrorists or are reluctant to act against terrorists will suffer. Even after the JI cells were detected and neutralized in Singapore, Malaysia and in the Philippines, President Megawatti placed her personal and political career before national and regional security and therefore, was hesitant to target the al-Qaeda network in Indonesia. Even after Bali, Indonesia is targeting only JI members directly connected to the Bali bomb blast. Indonesia is neither targeting JI as an organization nor its political wing, Mujahideen Council of Indonesia led by Abu Bakar Bashir, and its militia wing, Lashkar Jundullah, led by Agus Dwikarna. Lashkar Jundullah was responsible for bombing the McDonalds in Makassar, Sulawesi, Indonesia on 6 December 2002. The bombing killed three Indonesians, including the bomber, and injured several.[13] As a result, JI and Lashkar Jundullah will be able to strike again, both inside Indonesia and using Indonesia as a launching pad, its neighbouring countries.

PROGNOSIS

Despite being the most hunted movement in history, al-Qaeda and its associated organisations will pose a significant threat in the immediate term (1-2 years). Al-Qaeda per se will fragment, decentralise, regroup in five zones of the world, work with like-minded groups, select a wider range of targets, focus on economic targets and population centres, and conduct most attacks in the global south. Although the group will be constrained from conducting coordinated simultaneous attacks against high profile

[13] "Three Killed in McDonald Blast", CNN, 6 December 2002.

symbolic or strategic targets in the West, together with its regional counterparts al-Qaeda will conduct similar attacks in Asia, Africa, Middle East, and even in Latin America. Despite heavy losses, including the likely capture or death of its core and penultimate leaders, al-Qaeda's anti-Western universal Jihad ideology inculcated among the politicised and radicalised Muslims will sustain support for Islamism, Islamist political parties and Islamist terrorist groups. With the detection, disruption and degradation of its human and material infrastructure, al-Qaeda may evolve and survive as a state-of-mind among Islamist territorial and migrant pockets. With a skewed US Middle Eastern policy, Islamist support for political violence will grow prompting terrorist groups to conduct mass casualty attacks, especially suicide bombings of economic targets and population centres.

To compensate for the loss of its state-of-the-art operational and training infrastructure, al-Qaeda will change its shape. Although its intention to attack has not diminished, its capability to attack has suffered gravely. With the US working with several Middle Eastern and Asian governments, al-Qaeda's strength has depleted to a third of its rank and file, especially through the loss or capture of its key leaders and experienced operatives. Therefore, the group is increasingly probing targets that can be attacked with the least effort and at least cost. In keeping with its doctrine of repeating its successes, al-Qaeda and its associate groups are increasingly adopting the tactic of suicide terrorism against soft targets.

While al-Qaeda's priority will be attack US targets, it only has the resources and opportunity to attack US allies and friends. With diminished al-Qaeda assets and hardened US and Israeli diplomatic targets, the group will attempt to mount attacks against British, French, German, Italian, Canadian and Australian targets and possibly other European and Japanese targets. Throughout 2002, al-Qaeda or its associate groups killed German tourists in Djerba, Tunisia, French naval technicians in Karachi, Pakistan, Australians and Westerners in Bali, Indonesia, and Israelis Mombassa, Kenya. Osama bin Laden's pronouncements in October and November 2002 will be the best guide to unfolding al-Qaeda events in 2003. As such more effort is needed to track and target al-Qaeda experts moving worldwide and prevent them from coordinating attacks together with al-Qaeda associate groups with which they had shared ideology, finance and training during the last decade in Afghanistan and in other conflict zones.

Countermeasures, especially target hardening, by law enforcement and protective services of vulnerable government personnel and infrastructure have forced al-Qaeda to focus on economic targets and population centres. Hardening of government targets will displace the threat to softer targets making civilians prone to terrorist attacks. Economic targets, especially the tourist and the hotel industry will suffer from terrorism. Churches, synagogues and other non-Islamic institutions as well as trade and investment will remain particularly vulnerable. Similarly, hardening of land and aviation targets will shift the threat to sea targets particularly to commercial maritime targets. Due to the difficulty of hijacking aircraft to ram them against targets difficult to acquire from surface attacks, al-Qaeda will acquire and employ hand held Surface-to-Air Missiles (SAMs). If appropriate and immediate countermeasures are not taken to target the al-Qaeda shipping network, SAMs under al-Qaeda control held in the Pakistan-Kashmir-Afghanistan theatre, the Arabian Peninsula and the Horn of Africa will find their way to the Far East and to Europe, and possibly even to North America. Other groups operationally and ideologically unconnected to al-Qaeda will learn from al-Qaeda technologies, tactics and techniques.

With US security forces and the intelligence community targeting al-Qaeda's nerve centre in Afghanistan-Pakistan, al-Qaeda will decentralise even further. While its organisers of attacks will remain in Pakistan and its immediate neighbourhood, its operatives will travel back and forth coordinating with al-Qaeda nodes in the south. To make its presence felt, al-Qaeda will increasingly rely on its global terrorist network of like-minded groups in Southeast Asia, south Asia, Horn of Africa, Middle East and the Caucasus to strike its enemies. Already attacks in Kenya, Indonesia, India, Pakistan, Kuwait and Yemen seek to compensate for the loss and lack of space and opportunity to operate in Afghanistan. Its operatives will work together with JI and other groups in Southeast Asia, Al Ithihad al Islami in the Horn of Africa, Chechen Mujahideen in the Caucasus and the Transcaucasus, Tunisian Combatants Group and other groups in the Middle East, Jaish-e-Mohommad and other groups in South Asia. Al-Qaeda will rely on groups it had trained and financed in the past decade to continue the fight. In addition to its own members, al-Qaeda will operate through the Salafi Group for Call and Combat (GSPC) and Takfir Wal Hijra—two groups it had infiltrated in Europe and North America. With the transfer of terrorist technology and expertise from the centre to the periphery, the attacks by the associated groups of al-Qaeda will pose a threat as great as that of al-Qaeda.

Although attacking inside North America, Europe, Australasia and Israel remains a priority, the measures and countermeasures taken by these governments will make it difficult for al-Qaeda to mount an operation in the West. Al-Qaeda finds it less costly to operate in parts of Asia, Africa, and the Middle East where there is lack of security controls. Therefore, most attacks will be against Western targets located in the global south. While focusing on Western targets will remain a priority, al-Qaeda will continue to conduct operations against Muslim rulers and regimes supporting the US-led 'war on terror'. The physical security of Pakistani and Afghan leaders Musharraf and Karzai will remain particularly vulnerable and their regimes will come under sustained political challenges. While a number of Pakistani groups fighting in Kashmir will come under greater control of the al-Qaeda, the group working together with the surviving elements of the Taliban will develop a clandestine network inside Afghanistan to conduct guerrilla warfare, terrorism and political assassinations.

For greater impact, al-Qaeda will conduct coordinated simultaneous attacks against symbolic, high prestige or strategic targets with the intention of inflicting maximum damage to human and physical infrastructure. With al-Qaeda resources under strain and its operatives coming under increasing scrutiny in the global north, al-Qaeda will be constrained from mounting multiple attacks in the global north. However, al-Qaeda and its associate groups are still able to mount multiple operations in the global south where they have greater leverage, space and time to operate. For instance, JI attacked Sari and Kuta clubs and the US consulate in Bali, Indonesia on 12 October 2002; and al-Qaeda attacked an Israeli owned hotel and aircraft in Mombassa, Kenya on 29 November 2002.

Al-Qaeda has suffered with the arrest of nearly 3000 organisers, operatives and supporters worldwide from October 2001. With the increase in pressure, the surviving operatives of al-Qaeda are increasingly depending on its associate groups to conduct attacks. Traditionally, al-Qaeda with better trained, more experienced and highly committed operatives wanted to attack more difficult targets especially strategic targets and leave the easier and tactical targets to its associated groups. Today, with al-Qaeda operatives working closely together, the lethality of the attacks conducted by the associate groups of al-Qaeda is increasing. As Bali demonstrated, the attacks conducted by the associate groups of al-Qaeda can be as lethal as the attacks conducted by al-Qaeda itself. With attacks conducted by al-Qaeda's associated groups posing a threat as great as that al-Qaeda, the theatre of war will widen. US assistance, presence and influence will grow in the Muslim World generating wide-ranging reactions.

With the loss of Afghanistan as a "liberated theatre of Jihad", Islamists will seek to create new theatres. Dr Zawahiri considers

Afghanistan and Chechnya as the only two liberated theatres of Jihad.[14] Already due to the difficulty of movement of recruits and flow of support from Islamist migrant pockets in the West and in the Middle East to Afghanistan, there has been a partial diversion of support to Chechnya. Although there is a significant reserve of Afghan trained active and sleeper terrorists in the West, terrorists entering the West to attack Western targets may be trained in a number of theatres especially Chechnya. With al-Qaeda fragmenting, several other groups will take over the role of waging a universal Jihad. More territorial Islamist groups will espouse universal agendas and more Muslim separatist groups will become vulnerable to penetration by Islamist groups.

Al-Qaeda will be operating across the technological spectrum but is likely to use low-tech high-impact attacks, especially civilian infrastructure to attack civilian society and critical infrastructure. With greater border controls, members and associate members of al-Qaeda will use what can be readily purchased off the shelf especially from pharmacies, chemist shops, and hardware stores. Al-Qaeda members will live off the environment and turn commercially available material into weapons. Al-Qaeda's Tunisian member conducted a suicide attack against the oldest Jewish synagogue in Djerba, Tunisia, using a LPG truck; JI used a consignment of chlorate purchased from the port city of Surabaya in Indonesia against targets in Bali; and 9/11 hijackers used passenger aircraft against America's icons. The latter attack, an al-Qaeda detainee said was "like using your own finger to prick your eye." Using multiple identities, al-Qaeda members will travel to target countries, receive instructions, plan and prepare attacks through the Internet, and attack targets. They will generate support from low level crime, organised crime, infiltrated charities, and from politicised and radicalised segments of their migrant and diaspora communities.

[14]Ayman al-Zawahiri, "Knights Under the Prophet's Banner—Mediations on the Jihadist Movement", London: AL Sharq al-Awsat (in Arabic), 2 December 2001.

As per the method used by Khalid Sheikh Mohammad the former head of the military committee of al-Qaeda the pattern of attacks could become: First, mass casualty attacks, second, the abundant use of suicide terrorism, third, bombings, and fourth, assassination. As mass casualty attacks need a large number of operatives, greater resources and planning over a long period of time, al-Qaeda will be able to conduct fewer attacks but they are likely to become spectaculars or theatrical attacks. Assassination will be used more frequently although suicide bombings will be the most predominant form of attack. As suicide attacks are very difficult to disrupt in the execution phase, 2003 will see the tactic of suicide terrorism being used more widely. As al-Qaeda maximises its successes and partial successes of attacks and minimises its failures, suicide attacks will become increasingly common. Although al-Qaeda's long-term and sustained interest to use chemical, biological, radiological and nuclear agents has not diminished, conventional terrorism will remain the preferred mode of attack.

STATE RESPONSE

The fight against al-Qaeda and its associate groups seriously began only after 9/11. Although the JI network in Southeast Asia was detected in December 2001, only some countries acknowledged that JI was a threat until the JI bombing of Bali. Indonesia until Bali and Thailand even after Bali, lived in denial of the very existence of a regional terrorist network. Although al-Qaeda in Southeast Asia has a head start of ten years, government actions against both al-Qaeda and its associate groups have significantly damaged their capabilities. A year after 9/11, al-Qaeda remains a threat to Southeast Asian governments and societies. Largely due to the tireless efforts of the intelligence community especially of the Singaporean security service, the region is aware of the existence of a resilient terrorist network. Only about a fourth of the operatives have suffered arrest or death. Although parts of the network have suffered extensive damage, such as its Singaporean, Malaysian and Filipino components, the organisation's leadership; support (propaganda, recruitment, fund raising, procurement, transportation, safe houses); and operational (surveillance, attack) organs are fully functional. Only a regional approach involving all the countries by firstly acknowledging the presence of a pervasive group and thereafter its potentiality for damaging society and country can prompt the region to comprehensive and sustained action. Since 9/11, regional security and intelligence agencies are rapidly developing a reasonably good understanding of the terrorist network—its functionaries, its assets, its linkages, and its *modus operandi.* Initially, some leaders did not wish to take an aggressive stand and action against al-Qaeda and JI stating that the terrorists only targeted the US. through trial and tribulation, political leaders in Malaysia and Indonesia are realizing that the policy of appeasement with the Islamists does not work.

As JI is a pan-Southeast Asian organization operating across territorial borders, only the creation of a regional task force can cripple JI as an organisation. Whenever JI has been targeted in one country its operatives and assets have moved to the neighbouring country. For instance, when 240 JI members of Malaysia were targeted, the bulk of its operatives moved to Indonesia and to Thailand. The nature of the JI organization is such that no one single country can successfully fight and dismantle it. The targeting of JI must be intelligence driven, primarily based on human source intelligence, detainee debriefs and intercepted communications. While intelligence agencies provide the critical intelligence, law enforcement authorities must hunt down JI members, especially the leaders that provide strategic and tactical direction and the handful of experts who coordinate financial, logistical and other operations. The key to fighting JI is common counter-terrorism intelligence databases, exchange of personnel, transfer of expertise, joint operations, and most importantly, sharing of experience. By relentlessly targeting the core and penultimate leaders of JI, governments must develop robust political and economic responses to isolate their existing and potential supporters.

Prophylactic measures must prevent the JI support base from growing. When hunted, JI's resilience is dependent on its ability to replenish its human losses and material wastage. The milieu in which JI operates provides significant recruits and support at this point of time. As long as governments can prevent the socio-economic and political marginalisation of the Muslim communities in their countries, JI will find it difficult to survive. Therefore, the highest priority must be given to prevent the demonisation of the Muslim community especially if they are migrants in countries such as Australia. Like in the case of other religious communities, it must always be remembered that it is a miniscule proportion of Muslims who support violence.

The fight against JI must be comprehensive, not only military. That is, within the Muslim communities a clear message must be sent that JI is not Koranic but a heretical organization. Like al-Qaeda, JI misinterprets and misrepresents the Koran to advance its political aims and objectives. Unlike the military response, the ideological response will take more time to take effect, but it is by far the most effective. It will not only disrupt the flow of recruits and reduce support but also generate high grade and high quality information about JI that could be exploited by governments to target JI capabilities. As JI is a multidimensional organization, the response to JI must be multipronged. JI capabilities cannot be degraded and destroyed militarily alone. It is a multiagency effort involving the customs, immigration, coast guard, police, military, intelligence services, community organisations, religious institutions, schools and the mass media. The average life span of a terrorist group is 13.5 years.[15] It is a long fight, but with determination, commitment and unity of purpose at all levels, especially at the political level, it is a fight that can be won.

[15]Research conducted by Alex Schmid and Albert Jongman, PIOOM, The Netherlands, 1998-2000.

As much as 2002 was, 2003 will be a year of experience and learning both for government law enforcement and intelligence agencies. With the wider acknowledgement that there is no standard textbook for fighting the al-Qaeda, it will be a learning process where new structures and institutions will have to be built and shaped to fight a rapidly evolving, cunning and ruthless foe, willing to kill and to die. To win, governments will have to repeat their successes and build upon their successes. Past experience suggests that the fight against terrorism is a prolonged battle requiring patience and commitment. The fight against al-Qaeda—a hydra-headed entity that has proved its resilience repeatedly—cannot be an exception. Since 9/11, the dent and damage to al-Qaeda at all levels has only been partial. The global organisation has suffered significant damage, but the threat has not diminished. Although al-Qaeda's military commander Mohammad Atef alias Abu Hafs and Abu Zubaidah has been captured and killed, the 9/11 mastermind Khalid Shaik Mohammed (uncle of Ramzi Ahmed Yousef), and chief of finance Mustafa Ahmed Al Hawasawi are still free. These highly experienced and committed "experts" are planning and preparing for the next operation.

Al-Qaeda has suffered gravely in Afghanistan and partially elsewhere, but the core leadership is alive and the group's ideology is intact. The dozen attacks and fresh propaganda indicate that the leadership as well as the members has not given up the fight. To nurture existing and rekindle new Muslim migrant and territorial support, al-Qaeda on 10 September 2002 issued a 100-paged document seeking to justify why they struck America's most outstanding landmarks on 11 September 2001. Amidst security countermeasures the group has demonstrated its capacity to replicate, regenerate and reorganise.

In Southeast Asia, al-Qaeda cells are probing the gaping holes in the post—9/11 security architecture in order to strike. Wherever there are resources and opportunity al-Qaeda super cells will strike.

Today, no one single country can protect itself from a multinational terrorist organisation. For instance, Malaysia, Indonesia and Singapore cannot protect themselves as long as al-Qaeda has a robust presence in Indonesia. The first step towards reducing the immediate threat to Southeast Asia is to develop a regional task force to target al-Qaeda's support and operational infrastructure at home and in the immediate neighbourhood.

CONCLUSION

With persistence and perseverance, al-Qaeda as a physical entity can be destroyed. As long as its ideology remains appealing, al-Qaeda will pose a continuous terrorist threat to governments and societies worldwide. Although al-Qaeda as a physical entity will be relegated to history in the next few years, it has at least partially accomplished its primary role of "showing the way" to other groups, especially the need to go beyond a limited territorial agenda and wage a universal Jihad. Such an appealing ideology cannot be countered in the short term. The momentum al-Qaeda has so successfully unleashed will spawn and sustain a dozen existing and emerging Islamist groups at least in the mid-term (5 years).

US policies towards the Middle East, especially the unilateral US invasion of Iraq and Israeli-Palestinian issue will strengthen support for Islamism, Islamist political parties and terrorist groups. The US's skewed foreign policy will continue to pose a significant terrorist threat to Western interests both at home and overseas. In many countries, Islamism will move from the periphery to the centre, making it difficult for many governments to openly support the US-led "War against terrorism." With support for Islamism rising, Islamists will campaign either politically or violently or both in Turkey, Pakistan, Indonesia, and other emerging democracies. In addition to well-organised groups, individual terrorists will mount operations, similar to the shooting at the El Al counter at the Los Angeles Airport on America's Independence Day 2002. With more news in the media about Islam, the Muslim public will become more aware of Islam. The number of Muslims directly supporting violence will remain very small but there will be more support for a Muslim way of life, especially the implementation of Sharia laws. Furthermore, the need to wage Jihad in support of their suffering brethren will rise among politicised and radicalised segments of the Muslims.

If the threat posed by Islamism is to be countered and the life span of Islamist terrorist groups is to be shortened in the long-term (10 years), the current Western, especially the US approach of 95 per cent military and 5 per cent ideological will have to be reversed. To reduce the space for the al-Qaeda to survive and grow, the international community must develop a multipronged, multidimensional, multiagency, and multijurisdictional approach against terrorism. Failure to develop a comprehensive long-term strategic response will mean, al-Qaeda changing shape, surviving and continuing the fight.

CHAPTER 7

Can the Taliban be Disciplined?

Sreedhar

Since they started ruling Afghanistan from Kabul in September 1996, the Taliban committed three major tactical mistakes. Their abuse of Saudi Arabia, the custodian of the holy places of Islam, resulted in the Saudis lowering their support to the Taliban considerably. Second, the hijackers of Indian Airlines Flight 814 from Kathmandu to New Delhi were not punished according to the law of the Islamic Emirates of Afghanistan, which convinced the international community that a nexus existed between the Taliban and the terrorists. Along with this, the drought in Afghanistan in 1999-2000 and the repressive rule of the Taliban created a backlash. There were regular reports in the media about how the Taliban were losing their control. Last, in a moment of bravado in January 2000, they recognised the Chechnyan dissident movement.

In addition, the neighbourhood of the Islamic Emirates of Afghanistan has turned hostile to the Taliban. A concerted effort is on among the neighbouring countries to tame the present leadership of the Taliban and bring in moderates to the centre stage in Afghanistan. In this effort, Iran is playing a major role by mobilising all anti-Taliban forces within Afghanistan on to a single platform. Simultaneously, efforts are on in the same direction by the Central Asian states, China, Russia and even the US, the creator and mentor of the Taliban movement. Pakistan, being caught in an economic and political mess internally, is not able to bale out the Taliban from this hostile environment. Pakistan is faithfully following the demands being made by other countries to curb the Taliban.

Whether these efforts succeed or not is an open-ended question. To succeed, the international community has to come out with a plan of what to do with the jihadi *forces being trained by the Taliban. No one seems to have a ready answer.*

On 26/27 September 2000, the Taliban complete four years of their rule from Kabul. The first five years saw the Taliban 'defeating' one Afghan warlord after another, with some occasional setbacks, which they were able to overcome. Even though they were not recognised diplomatically by the international community (with the exception of Pakistan, Saudi Arabia and the UAE), the lines of communications with the Taliban were kept open by almost everyone. All this seems to have suddenly changed from December 1999. The way the Taliban handled the hijacking of Indian Airlines Flight 814 from Kathmandu (Nepal) to New Delhi on 24 December 1999, suddenly robbed them of their image of being the good Muslims which they claim to be. The manner in which they escorted the hijackers and the terrorists released from Indian prisons to the Pak-Afghan border in the swap deal made many wonder about the Taliban's bona fides. The hijackers receiving arms and ammunition from the Taliban during the time the hijacked plane was parked in Kandahar, considerably alienated the international public opinion.[1] *The Taliban's unwillingness to try and punish the hijackers according to the law of the Islamic Emirates of Afghanistan lent credence to the linkage between them and terrorist outfits operating in and around South West Asia. The claim of the Taliban and their mentors in Pakistan that their conduct was correct did not cut much ice with international public opinion. Their argument that Osama Bin Laden would be subjected to the law of the land if evidence was found against him, sounded hollow.*

Another tactical mistake the Taliban made was ridiculing the Saudi monarchy. There were reports in the international media that in a meeting between Saudi intelligence chief, Prince Turki and Mullah Umar, the latter in insulted him, and even abused the House

[1] 'Relief and Surrender', *India Today*, 10 January 2000, pp. 31-66.

of Sauds. This automatically brought a sharp reaction from the Saudis. They reduced their diplomatic presence in Kabul to the bare minimum, and started treating the Taliban movement as an exclusively Pakistani affair. This disrespect to the custodians of the holy shrines of Islam also reduced the Taliban's clout in the Islamic world.[2]

Last, the Taliban's recognition of the Chechnyan rebel movement in January 2000 brought its confrontation with Russia into the open. Consequently, the neighbouring Central Asian states strengthened their defences against Afghanistan to counter any Taliban mischief. The Taliban, thus, unwittingly brought the Central Asian states (which were distancing themselves from Russia), together.[3]

These three tactical mistakes by the Taliban leadership resulted in a coordinated effort by anti-Taliban forces in Afghanistan and the immediate neighbours of Afghanistan to start a process of disciplining the Taliban.

It is proposed to examine here how opposition to the Taliban rule is surfacing since the beginning of January 2000, and some of the measures being taken by the neighbouring countries to tame the Taliban.

OPPOSITION TO THE TALIBAN

Reports from Taliban-controlled Afghanistan indicate that all is not well there since January 2000. First, there was a report of a rebellion by a group of tribal leaders from Paktiya, Khost and Paktika against the Taliban administration. They issued a 15-day ultimatum to the Taliban authorities on 21 January demanding return of government land which was being sold by Taliban officials based on forged documents, failing which they threatened to launch a holy war

[2]Bhandara, M. P. 2000, 'Taliban and Pak: The Tail Wags the Dog', *Down* (reproduced in *The Asian Age*). 17 May.

[3]For an excellent background of the Taliban's recognition of Chechnya as a separate republic, see Brig. Vinod Anand, 2000, 'Export of Holy Terror to Chechnya From Pakistan and Afghanistan', *Strategic Analysis*, 24 (3): 539-52. June.

against the Taliban. They also wanted accounts of the tax revenues collected by the Taliban. According to *Sahaar*, a Pakistan-based Afghan newspaper, the tribal leaders in Khost were the most dissatisfied group.[4]

This was followed by the hijacking of an Ariana Boeing 727 with 178 people on board on 6 February during a domestic flight from Kabul to Mazar-e-Sharif. Initial reports about the hijacking indicated that the hijackers wanted Gen. Ismail Khan and three others to be released.

Though the hijacking drama ended peacefully after a week, yet some of the details were alarming. There were reports in the Pakistani press that the weapons for the hijackers were smuggled in by some female passengers.[5] Most of the passengers, after getting off at a suburban London airport, sought political asylum in England. Mullah Umar and his comrades, who claimed that the Afghan people welcomed their rule, suddenly got exposed. To a certain extent, the hijacking drama undermined the authority of the Taliban leadership, specially Mullah Umar's. It also exposed the extent to how his rule is forcing people to find escape routes through hazardous means.

Then came the news of the escape of the former Governor of Herat, Gen. Ismail Khan, along with three other anti-Taliban forces' leaders, from a high-security prison in Kandahar on 26 March.[6] Though there are contradicting reports about where these four men are taking shelter, it is quite clear their escape could not have taken place without the active connivance of some senior personnel in the Taliban hierarchy. A massive operation to cover up this security lapse seems to have started with the disappearance of Hikmatullah, who allegedly helped Ismail Khan and others in the jailbreak. Interestingly

[4] '*Afghanistan*', *Asian News Digest*, 26 February-4 March 2000, p. 129.

[5] Yusufzai, Rahimullah. 2000. 'Flight to the West', *The News on Sunday* (Islamabad). 13 February. For a detailed report on the harsh economic conditions in Kabul, see Zahid Hussain, 2000, 'Life Among the Ruins', *Newsline*, pp. 64-66.

[6] Yusufzai, Rahimullah. 2000. 'Ismail Claims to be in the West', *The News*, 3 April.

enough, this is reported to be the second attempt by these four to escape. In an earlier attempt, three other important political prisoners, Abdul Hakim Zarba (a former military commander belonging to the minority Shia Hazara community), another military commander, Ahmadullah (who hailed from Arghandab in Kandahar province and had served Burhanuddin Rabbani's government), and one Abdul Quayyum managed to escape.[7]

This year's 26 March jailbreak has also come in the wake of a similar incident which reportedly took place in Khost, wherein several prisoners escaped from Khost prison during the Eid-ul Azha holidays.[8]

While the Taliban authorities were trying to overcome the shock of the jailbreak, nine days later, on 4 April, Mohammad Arif Khan, Governor of Kunduz province in Northern Afghanistan who was on a visit to Peshawar (NWFP), was killed by unidentified gunmen in broad daylight.[9]

It may be recalled that Arif Khan spent all his life fighting for the Afghan cause. Initially, he fought against the Red Army, then he took on Hizbul Mujahideen groups single-handedly before joining the Taliban in 1997. Many observers of the Afghan civil war believe that his joining the Taliban tilted the balance of power in their favour. He converted Kunduz province into a Taliban bastion. In fact, after joining the Taliban, Arif Khan along with another Pushtoon commander, Bashir Baghlani, saved a large Taliban force which was trapped by the Northern Alliance forces. They later regrouped and captured some of the neighbouring provinces like Takhar, Baghlan, Samagan and Balkh.

For this extraordinary loyalty towards them, the Taliban's

[7] *Ibid.* Also see Rahimullah Yusufzai, 2000, 'Conflicting Reports about Ismail whereabouts', *The News*, 30 March.

[8] *Ibid.* Also see Rahimullah Yusufzai, 2000, 'Taliban Launches Manhunt for Ismail Whereabouts', *The News*, 30 March.

[9] Khan, Ismail. 2000. 'Afghan Governor, Guard Shot Dead in Peshawar', *The News*, 5 April.

supreme leader, Mullah Umar, retained Arif Khan as the governor of Kunduz. 'This was probably the first time that a mujahideen commander was retained in his office in his native province by the Taliban and allowed to keep his arms and men.'[10]

Two days before the killing of Arif Khan, Iranian news agency IRNA reported that one of the Taliban commanders, Mullah Sher Mohammad Akund along with 30 colleagues in Kunduz, sought shelter from the Northern Alliance after his clash with local Taliban forces.

Besides these developments, Taliban-controlled Afghanistan had been experiencing regular bomb blasts. In February 2000, a bomb blast at Kabul airport destroyed a Taliban jet fighter.[11] Again, in May, an ammunition dump in the Taliban's 17th Division military headquarters in Kabul's northern Khair Khana neighbourhood exploded. Though no casualties were reported, Divisional Commander Mullah Habibullah blamed the Northern Alliance, calling it 'an act of sabotage by our enemies'.[12]

Simultaneously, reports from Kandahar and Islamabad started making the rounds saying that serious differences had developed between the rulers of Pakistan and the Taliban, specially due to the latter's leanings towards Osama Bin Laden. These reports got further credence with a report in a Peshawar-based Pushto daily (*Wahdat*) coming out with a story on 3 March, that a new group was emerging in Afghanistan to replace the Taliban. Tentatively, it is being called the 'Islamic Shura for Reconciliation and Liberation of Afghanistan'. Sharatte, a leader of the Jamiat Islami from Laghman province of Afghanistan, is being considered its new leader.

Although all these incidents are not connected with each other, they do indicate some definite trends. Even though the Taliban authorities and their sympathisers in the Pakistani media want

[10]Yusufzai, Rahimullah. 2000. 'Killing of Afghans Challenge to Law Enforcing Agencies', *The News*, 5 April.

[11]AP report, 'Bomb Blast in Kabul', *The Asian Age*, 27 May 2000.

[12]Reuter report, 'Explosion Rocks Taliban Military Base', *The News*, 27 May 2000.

outsiders to believe that the Taliban are consolidating their position, the ground realities seem to be the other way around. Mullah Umar is not a charismatic leader like Gen. Ismail Khan and Ahmed Shah Masood. The latter might not be at the helm of affairs today, but they became part and parcel of Afghan folklore. Therefore, Mullah Umar seems to be incapable of commanding the respect, authority and loyalty of the people of Afghanistan.

Equally important is that Mullah Umar and the Taliban captured all the power centres. By 26/27 September 2000, they will complete four years in Kabul, the crucial centre of power in Afghanistan. Their rule has made no difference to the common man's life. If anything, it has made his life more difficult because of Mullah Umar's desire to impose his own version of Sụnni Islam. The regime is not recognised by the international community with the exception of Pakistan, Saudi Arabia and the UAE. Even the international aid agencies are not allowed to operate freely, as the Taliban perceive their activities as being against the tenets of Sunni Islam, as interpreted by them. The apologists of the Taliban in Pakistan argue that Mullah Umar and his government are not educated in modern statecraft, and that they will need time to learn. Up to a point, the common man in Kabul or Kandahar went along with this reasoning. But not he feels that the Taliban are not willing to learn.

NEIGHBOUR'S INITIATIVES

IRAN

The Taliban got cornered by well-coordinated efforts by all their neighbours (other than Pakistan). At one level, the Iranians played a decisive role in strengthening anti-Taliban forces. From November 1999, there were regular reports in the international media about how Iran was pouring in millions of dollars worth of arms and ammunition to the Ahmed Shah Masood forces. Arms supplies from Iran reach them by traversing Turkmenistan, Uzbekistan and southern Tajikistan from where they are sent by road across the Amu

Darya (river) to northern Afghanistan. In this process, Iran seems to be coordinating its efforts with others (including Russia) in supplying arms to Ahmed Shah Masood.

Simultaneously, in March 2002, Iran also tried and succeeded in bringing together two major Uzbek factions, one led by Gen. Abdul Rashid Dostum and the other by Gen. Abudullah Malik. In the now-famous meeting held in Meshad, close to Iran's border with Afghanistan, both leaders agreed to go back to Afghanistan and rally Uzbek forces opposing the Taliban.[13]

In an equally important move, the Iranians managed a meeting between Dostum and Masood in March 2000, in Termezia in southern Uzbekistan. Both are reported to have agreed on renewing military cooperation. The Iranians also managed to beef up the anti-Taliban forces among the Shia Hazaras in Hazarajat in Central Afghanistan.[14]

Along with mobilising anti-Taliban forces, Iran also stepped up its diplomatic efforts to isolate the Pakistan-Taliban combine. The Taliban leadership's intransigence at the OIC/UN-sponsored Jeddah talks alienated them considerably within the Islamic world. Having succeeded in isolating the Taliban, Iran stepped up its border trade that started in November 1999, to keep the lines of communications open with the Taliban, and drive a wedge between the Taliban and Pakistan. To make its intentions clear to the Taliban that they could mobilise public opinion in the Islamic world, Iran quietly invited the Burhanuddin Rabbani faction to the ECO summit in Teheran in June 2000.[15]

At another level, Iran too started its own brand of peace initiatives by mobilising overseas Afghans. For the time being, Iran does not seem to be too enthusiastic about the initiative of King

[13] Rashid, Ahmed. 2000. 'Iran Rebuilds Anti-Taliban Alliance', *The Nation* (Islamabad). 4 April.

[14] *Ibid.*

[15] *Ibid.* Also see NNI report, 2000, 'Taliban Flay ECO Invitation to Rabbani', 10 June.

Zahir Shah to succeed, as its success may have repercussions on Teheran's domestic polity.[16]

THE CENTRAL ASIAN STATES

The Taliban's ideology, and its efforts to establish an Islamic *ummah* are anathema to the Central Asian leaders. This becomes evident from their willingness to seek help from every quarter, including Russia and the US. Their seeking outside help is understandable, as these countries have no capacity to challenge cross-border terrorism from the highly motivated and battle-hardened Taliban. The presence of a charismatic leader like Osama Bin Laden and his access to a reasonable amount of resources cannot be challenged by these underdeveloped states. The Central Asian leadership was alarmed at the bomb blasts in early 1999 in Tashkent and the proposed assault on Farghana Valley from the Islamic Movement of Uzbekistan activists.[17]

In fact, some reports even suggested that the threat posed by 1,200 Uzbek militants based in northern Afghanistan and another 600 based in Tajikistan to topple Uzbek President Karimov, started ringing alarm bells all around Central Asia. These militants, regularly supplied arms by the Taliban officials and funded by Osama Bin Laden and the narcotic trade mafia, have enlisted Tajiks, Arabs, Uighurs, Chechens and Pakistanis in their ranks.[18]

What the Taliban never anticipated is that the Central Asian states would approach Russia and the US for assistance, and that both would readily oblige. One interpretation could be that the Russo-US differences on a variety of issues, made the Taliban conclude that they would not act in unison. The Taliban are also under the impression that having defeated Russia once, it would not be difficult for them to 'teach Moscow a lesson again'. Only with

[16]Reuter, *op. cit.*, n. 12 above.

[17]Rashid, Ahmed. 2000. 'US to Counter Terrorism in Afghanistan, C. Asia', *The Nation*, 4 May.

[18]*Ibid.*

that confidence did they recognise Chechnya in January 2000.

This over-confidence of the Taliban suddenly received a jolt when the Russian president's spokesman, Sergei Yastrzhenbsky, announced in May 2000 that Moscow was considering air strikes against Chechen rebel training camps in Afghanistan. He also disclosed that Chechen separatist leader Aslam Makhadov held meetings with Osama Bin Laden and Taliban officials in early May 2000. This Russian announcement received no condemnation from the US; according to unconfirmed reports, Washington even shared intelligence with Moscow. In fact, in a joint statement issued at the end of US Assistant Secretary of State Karl Inderfurth's visit to Moscow on 26 May, both sides expressed serious concern at the Afghan conflict and the 'Taliban's support to terrorism'.

CHINA

Equally significant is the subtle shift in the Chinese attitude towards the Taliban. In 1998 and 1999, China perceived that by engaging the Taliban, they would be able to contain the spread of Islamic radicalism in the sensitive Xinjiang Autonomous Region.[19] But they soon realised that the Taliban were not keeping up their part of the deal. The continued support extended by the Taliban to the 'Party of Allah', an organisation floated by the Xinjiang Muslims, created serious doubts about the Taliban's intentions.[20] In addition, the uncertainty being created by the Taliban in Central Asia has started affecting China's security interests in the region adversely. This made China come out publicly that Taliban-controlled Afghanistan was the source of instability in the South West Asian region.[21]

[19]See the chapter on China in Sreedhar and Mohinder Ved, 2000, *Afghan Buzkashi*, Delhi: Wordsmiths. For an excellent background on Islam in China, see Justine Ben-Adam, 1999, 'China', *Islam Outside the Arab World*, pp. 191-211. surrey: Curzon Press.

[20]Dhar, M. K. 2000. 'A Shanghai Forum with India', *The Pioneer*, 19 July.

[21]*Ibid.*

PAKISTAN

Pakistan, the staunch supporter of the Taliban since the beginning of the movement in 1994, has been in an economic and political mess for the last two years. Pakistan's problems got intensified with the fourth round of an Indo-Pakistan war, when it realised that to extricate the country from the economic and political mess in which it was mired, the international community's demand of distancing itself from the Taliban had to be accepted.

Therefore, Pakistan—which has no means to support them or rehabilitate them—has started distancing itself from the Taliban. Nawaz Sharif, days before he was deposed, accused the Taliban authorities of providing training to terrorists.[22] Gen. Pervez Musharraf repeated these charges during Mullah Rabbani's visit to Islamabad in January 2000. Even after announcing that he would visit Kandahar shortly in early February, Gen. Musharraf deferred the visit on one pretext or the other. His strategy of acquiring some pressure points on the Taliban leadership, by curtailing smuggling between the two countries and restricting trade to official channels, had already brought considerable resistance from Taliban sympathisers in NWFP, Baluchistan and Punjab.[23] Meanwhile, Pakistan also allowed the opening of a new UN office in Teheran to coordinate the work on Afghanistan. Reports from Islamabad say that this development may reduce the importance of the UN Special Representative's office in Islamabad. Though it is too early to come to any definite conclusion, all this indicates that the Taliban-Pakistan honeymoon seems to be running into rough weather.

On Gen. Pervez Musharraf's insistence, the Taliban 'closed down Rishkor Camp which had housed Pakistani and Arab militants'. Simultaneously, the Taliban also closed down another 18 terrorist

[22] 'Terrorists got Training in Afghanistan: PM 1999', *The Nation*, 8 October.

[23] Zulfikar, Raja. 2000. 'Pakistan, Afghanistan Condemn all Forms of Terrorism', *The News*, 2 February.

camps and rounded up an unspecified number of Arab extremists in June 2000.[24]

FRESH SANCTIONS AND DROUGHT

Against this backdrop of total isolation of the Taliban by the entire neighbourhood, fresh sanctions are being contemplated by the UN. The November 1999 UN sanctions froze all the Taliban's overseas assets, and prevented Taliban aircraft from flying abroad. The proposed sanctions, according to Ahmed Rashid,

> ... will attempt to create a virtual cordon sanitaire around Afghanistan to try and prevent weapon supplies from neighbouring countries flowing in and heroin flowing out. They will impose a trade embargo against the Taliban and demand extradition of thousands of foreigners fighting for the Taliban.[25]

Rashids adds that 'such sanctions will put enormous international pressure on Pakistan, whose madrassas supply thousands of volunteers to the Taliban. A possible trade embargo could decimate the smuggling trade, which Pakistan itself is trying to tackle, but revenues from which provide 60 percent of the Taliban's war budget.' In other words, if these sanctions materialise, the suffering and misery of the Afghan people under Taliban control would increase enormously. That may result in an internal upheaval in the Taliban leadership.[26]

Along with this, one has also to take into consideration the drought in Afghanistan. According to World Food Organisation (WFO) and Food and Agricultural Organisation (FAO) estimates, the drought of 1999-2000 reduced Afghan food production to 1.8

[24]Shaikh, Nizamuddin A. 2000. 'Terrorism is Still in the Headlines', *The News*, 6 June.

[25]Rashid, *op. cit.*, n. 17 above.

[26]*Ibid.*

million tons as against a normal 3-4 million tons. The report by the WFP/FAO says that in Afghanistan the rains normally start in October/November. Even if the precipitation improves in the next season, wheat harvests will not be available until May/June 2001. If the rains fail again, the situation's already catastrophic dimensions will worsen further.[27]

This grim situation was reflected in the Taliban's failure to launch any major summer offensive (as they had announced earlier) in May-June 2000 against their opponents. With their creator and mentor, Pakistan, distancing itself from them, the Taliban seem to be having few alternatives to falling in line with the wishes of the international community. That would include:

- giving up the idea of a Wahabi-Sunni Islamic *ummah*;
- giving up the power they acquired during the past four years;
- closing down of all terrorist training camps;
- handing over people like Osama Bin Laden to the countries where they are wanted; and
- bring down narcotics production considerably.

The question is, will the Taliban do it? The choices before them are getting narrower and narrower. It will be an extremely difficult exercise for people like Mullah Umar and his mentors to dismantle everything they created during these years. Countries like Pakistan which have nurtured and supported the Taliban and their brand of mercenaries, may have to face the effects of a backlash. Already, the Pakistan embassy in Kabul has been attacked and Pakistani sportsmen who were in Afghanistan on a 'friendly' visit were assaulted.

This apart, what is to be done with Afghan *jihadi* warriors, as the Taliban-trained militants are called? According to various estimates, their number varies from anything between 30,000 and 50,000. Disarmig them would be a distant dream. The Pakistani argument

[27]'Afghanistan Facing Acute Shortage of Food, says UN', *The Nation*, 10 June 2000.

of a need to make a distinction between terrorists and *jihadis* leaves doubts about Islamabad's intentions. If the foreigners among these *jihadis* warriors are repatriated to their respective countries—a suggestion floating around—most of them would face the death sentence. In fact, some countries from where these *jihadi* warriors originate may not even accept them. The other alternative could be that they be given Afghan citizenship, as and when peace returns to Afghanistan, and absorbed in the Afghan armed forces. They cannot be allowed to roam around in the region unchecked. Simultaneously, an international task force should monitor the dismantling of terrorist training camps both in Afghanistan and Pakistan and ensure they are not allowed to reopen.

All this will be relevant if the disciplining of the Taliban and their mentors, Pakistan, succeeds. This seems to be a direct challenge to the collective will of the international community.

CHAPTER 8

The Taliban Strike Back

B. Raman

Since August last, the situation in Afghanistan has been deteriorating. Increasing numbers of better trained, better equipped and better led Taliban cadres operating from sanctuaries in Pakistan have stepped up their hit-and-run raids into southern and eastern Afghanistan in order to demoralise the newly-raised army and police of the Hamid Karzai government in the hope of thereby inducing large-scale desertions. Their attacks have been focused on members of the new Afghan army, police and other government departments and foreign aid workers. They have avoided direct confrontations with the US forces, lest they pursue them into Pakistani territory. As a result, while there have been nearly 400 Afghan government and civilian fatal casualties, the number of fatal American casualties has been only four. The Taliban has also set up a well-run Psychological warfare (PSYWAR) machinery in Pakistan, which is used to add to the anti-US anger in Pakistan as well as Afghanistan. While the Hizb-e-Islami of Gulbuddin Hekmatyar has been operating jointly with the revived Taliban from Pakistani sanctuaries, the survivors of the al-Qaeda and the Pakistani components of the International Islamic Front (IIF) have been focusing on harassing the US troops in Iraq through well-motivated Jehadis infiltrated into Iraq through Iran or Saudi Arabia. The Pakistan-based Jehadi terrorists owing allegiance to bin Laden through the IIF have been calculating that if they maintain a low, but sustained level of violence in Afghanistan and Iraq without unduly provoking the Americans into massive retaliation, battle fatigue would set in and force the US government to recall its boys home before the campaign for the next year's presidential elections picks up momentum. Though the US has been saying that it is prepared for a longish stay, whatever be the cost in terms of funds and casualties, in both countries, the Jehadis view this as mere bravado and have convinced themselves that the closer the elections, the weaker will be the US will to continue the fighting. The USA's continued reluctance to act against Pakistan and make it pay a prohibitive price for helping the Jehadi terrorists is coming in the way of an effective counter-terrorism strategy. Encouraged by this US reluctance, the Pervez Musharraf regime continues to keep the Jehadi terrorists alive and active in the hope of using them to retrieve the lost Pakistani influence in Afghanistan and achieve its strategic objective of forcing a change in the status quo in India's Jammu and Kashmir.

7 October 2003 marked the second anniversary of the launching of what was code-named by the US as Operation Enduring Freedom. This code-name was given by the US to the operation launched by it in the Afghan territory against the Taliban, the al-Qaeda and the IIF for Jihad Against the Crusaders and the Jewish People, which was formed by Osama bin Laden in 1998, in association with 13 Jehadi terrorist organisations of the world, of whom five are presently from Pakistan.

The fact that the Taliban was fathered in 1994, when Benazir Bhutto was Pakistan's Prime Minister, by the Pakistani Ministry of the Interior and the Inter-Services Intelligence (ISI) is well known and the details relating to its birth and the subsequent spread of its control over 90 per cent of the Afghan territory, including Kabul, do not need recapitulation.

Similarly, the fact that initially the US had blessed the creation of the Taliban in the hope of thereby restoring order and internal security in Afghanistan and thus facilitating the project of the US oil company, UNOCAL, for the construction of oil and gas pipelines from Urkmenistan to Pakistan through Afghan territory is equally well known.

However, not so well known till recently was the role of the ISI and the Pakistan army in fathering even the al-Qaeda in the hope of using it for furthering Pakistan's strategic objectives in relation to Afghanistan and India. This has been brought out in an assessment prepared by the Defence Intelligence Agency (DIA) of the Pentagon on 24 September 2001, hardly 13 days after the al-Qaeda's terrorist strikes of 9/11 in US territory, which has been declassified recently by the US government, reportedly in response to an application under the Freedom of Information Act.

Many other documents of the DIA and the US State Department relating to Afghanistan have also been simultaneously declassified and these are available for perusal at the National Security Archives' web site at http://ww.gwu.edu/~nsarchiv/NSAEBB/NSAEBB97/index.htm.

The declassified DIA document of 24 September 2001 had carried the following damning account of Pakistan's role as the real hosts of bin Laden and his al-Qaeda in Afghanistan. It said: "Bin Laden's al-Qaeda network was able to expand under the safe sanctuary extended by Taliban following Pakistan directives. If there is any doubt in that issue, consider the location of bin Laden's camp targeted by US Cruise missiles (in August 1998), Zahawa. Positioned on the border between Afghanistan and Pakistan, it was built by Pakistani contractors, funded by Pakistan's Inter-Services Intelligence (ISI) Directorate and protected under the patronage of a local and influential Jadran tribal leader, Jalaluddin Haqqani. However, the real host in that facility was the Pakistani ISI. If this was later to become bin Laden's base, then serious questions are raised by the early relationship between bin Laden and Pakistan's ISI."

It described Jalaluddin Haqqani as "the Jadran tribal leader most exploited by ISI during the Soviet-Afghan war to facilitate the introduction of Arab mercenaries" and the Taliban as "the handy cloak woven by Pakistan to shroud their progress."

Thus, as the Pentagon was making the preparations for launching Operation Enduring Freedom, it was known even to its own experts in its intelligence community that the Pakistan army and its ISI were the creators and sponsors of not only the Taliban, but also of the al-Qaeda, which emerged as the most dreaded Jehadi terrorist organisation of the world after its head, Osama bin Laden, shifted from Sudan to Jalalabad in Afghanistan in 1996 from where he subsequently moved to Kandahar.

Despite this, the US chose to rely on the Pakistan army and its ISI for logistics and intelligence support in its operation to wipe out the Taliban, the al-Qaeda and the IIF. The army and Gen. Pervez Musharraf, Pakistan's military dictator, who had sponsored and used Jehadi terrorism in an attempt to achieve Pakistan's strategic objectives against India (destabilising India and annexing Jammu and Kashmir) and Afghanistan (strategic depth), were sought to be projected as the USA's stalwart ally in the war against terrorism and rewarded for their ostensible cooperation through the resumption of generous economic and military assistance, which had remained curtailed since the Pressler Amendment was invoked against Pakistan in 1990 for clandestinely developing a military nuclear capability and further cut after the Chagai nuclear tests of 1998 and the overthrow of the elected government headed by Nawaz Sharif, the then Prime Minister, by the army in October 1999.

Why did the US choose to rely on the sponsor of Jehadi terrorism in its attempt to vanquish it? There have been many answers to this question. None of them is totally satisfactory by itself, but all of them together give some indication of the thinking in Washington DC, which influenced the decision. Amongst such possible reasons mentioned by analysts, one could cite the following:

- The need for rear bases for the US armed forces in Pakistani territory from which they could operate in Afghan territory.
- The need for objective allies in the Pashtun community in the tribal belt on both sides of the Pakistan-Afghanistan border in its operations to eliminate Osama bin Laden and other leaders of the al-Qaeda.

- The need for intelligence support from the ISI because of the poor human intelligence (HUMINT) assets of the US intelligence community.
- The fear of a Talibanisation of Pakistan should the military be forced to go to the barracks and its role weakened. The army was wrongly perceived by the US not as the sponsor of the Jehadi forces, but as the bulwark in countering the spread of their influence.
- The belief that only the army would be able to prevent Pakistan's nuclear and missile assets from falling into the hands of the Jehadi terrorists.
- The US perception of Musharraf as a force for stability in Pakistan and as a Muslim with a modern outlook, who genuinely wanted to curb the fundamentalist forces in Pakistan.

Why did Musharraf choose to support the US in its attempts to neutralise the offspring of his own army and the ISI, thereby abandoning instruments which they had built up since 1994 for achieving what they looked upon as a strategic depth in Afghanistan and strengthening Pakistan's hold over that country? Musharraf, in his telecast to his people before 7 October 2001, cited two reasons for his *volte face*: namely, the importance of safeguarding Pakistan's strategic assets by which he meant its nuclear and missile capability and the need to maintain its capability for achieving its strategic objective on J&K against India.

In other words, he chose to abandon temporarily the gains which the Pakistan army had made in Afghanistan since 1994 through the Taliban and the al-Qaeda in order to protect Pakistan's nuclear and missile assets from any possible attempts at their neutralisation by the US and the retain the Army's ability to force a change in the status quo in J&K through the sponsorship of Jehadi terrorism. While thus abandoning at least temporarily the gains on the ground in Afghanistan, he took care to protect the instruments with which these gains had been made in the hope of using them again in future to retrieve the ground lost by Pakistan in Afghanistan.

Since 7 October 2001, the US military operations in Afghanistan have passed through three phases. In the first phase, the government set up by the Taliban with its administrative headquarters in Kabul and its religious headquarters in Kandahar was replaced by a provisional government headed by Hamid Karzai, an India-educated Pashtun enjoying the confidence of the US and other Western countries. In the second phase, the training and other terrorist infrastructure of the al-Qaeda and other components of the IIF in southern and eastern Afghanistan were destroyed through aerial and ground action. In the third phase, efforts were initiated to restore law and order and governance in the rural areas liberated from the control of the Jehadi terrorist forces and to build the infrastructure of a liberal democracy in the country in the form of a Constitution paving the way for free and fair elections by the following year.

REPLACING THE TALIBAN REGIME

Even though the undoubted success of the US-led coalition in the first phase was projected as due to the prowess of the US Armed Forces, it was largely due to the motivation and fighting capability of the forces of the Northern Alliance, which had been abandoned by the US and Pakistan after 1994 in favour of the Taliban. If India, Russia and Iran had not stood by the side of the late Ahmed Shah Masood and his Northern Alliance and helped it in whatever way they could, it is doubtful whether the post-Taliban Afghanistan would have had at its disposal the hard core of an army and an administration, which represented the positive aspects of Islam and sought to give it a modern outlook instead of taking Afghanistan back to the Middle Ages as the Pakistan and the US-supported Taliban sought to do.

It was shortsighted on the part of the US not to have recognised openly and handsomely the role of the Northern Alliance in helping in the liberation of the Afghan State and society from the stranglehold of the Taliban and its medieval mullahs. Not only that. In response to the sensitivities of Musharraf, who was afraid and continues to be so, that the Northern Alliance favoured the restoration of the historic friendly ties between Afghanistan and India, the US has at every stage tried to limit the influence of the leaders of the Northern Alliance on the ground that they were non-Pashtuns and hence would not enjoy the total confidence of the Pashtuns.

The attempts at State and administration re-building and to set up an all-ethnic army have also been influenced by an anxiety to restrict the influence of the Northern Alliance in the name of giving the Pashtuns their due share. The over-attention to the sensitivities of Musharraf and his anxiety to prevent the restoration of the historic ties of friendship between India and Afghanistan has also been responsible for the US action in having India excluded from any meaningful role in the International Security Assistance Force (ISAF), whose command and control have since been taken over by the NATO, and in training the new Afghan army.

If, in spite of the unhelpful attitude of the US and the obstructive policies of the Musharraf regime, the relations between India and Afghanistan have continued to develop in various fields, it has been largely due to the feelings of goodwill nursed by the Northern Alliance and Hamid Karzai himself towards India.

While Pakistan reconciled itself to the temporary loss of its ground influence in Afghanistan, it took care to give shelter to the leaders and cadres of the Taliban in its territory in the North-West Frontier Province (NWFP) and Balochistan and to help them re-group, re-train and re-arm in order to facilitate a come-back by the pro-Pakistan forces one day. Apart from a few individuals without any major importance such as Muttawakil, the former Taliban Foreign Minister, the former Ambassador of the Taliban in Islamabad, etc, who were handed over by Pakistan to the US forces for interrogation, it avoided arresting and handing over any Taliban leader (including its Amir Mullah Mohammad Omar) of importance to the US.

The US calculation that its uncritical support to the Musharraf regime would prevent any Talibanisation of Pakistan has already proved wrong. The coalition of six fundamentalist, pro-Taliban and pro-bin Laden parties called the Muttahida Majlis-e-Amal (MMA) managed to come to power in the NWFP on its own strength after the elections held in October the previous year. It is part of the ruling coalition in Balochistan in association with the pro-Musharraf Pakistan Muslim League (Qaid-e-Azam).

Never before in the parliamentary history of Pakistan had the fundamentalist parties done as well in any elections as they did last year. This was only partly due to the anti-US anger in the Pashtun belt because of the US action against the Taliban and alleged excesses by the US forces against the local people. It was largely due to Musharraf's own action in facilitating the victory of the fundamentalists by withdrawing pending cases under the anti-terrorism act against the candidates of the fundamentalist parties in order to enable them to contest the elections while he refused to withdraw even cases relating to white-collar crimes against mainstream leaders such as Benazir Bhutto, Nawaz Sharif, etc; by recognising the certificates in Islamic studies issued by the madrassas as equivalent to university degrees to enable the fundamentalist candidates circumvent the electoral provision that only graduates could contest the elections; and by engineering splits in the mainstream political parties critical of him in order to weaken them.

Musharraf's calculation in facilitating the fundamentalist victory was two-fold. First, to convey a message to the US that if it continued to press him to act against the Jehadi terrorists operating against India, there was a danger of the fundamentalist influence spreading to the rest of the country and second, to use the fundamentalist control of the key provinces in the tribal belt as an alibi for explaining his inability to stop the flow of local support to the Taliban and the al-Qaeda.

After the fundamentalist coalition came to power in the NWFP and Balochistan, the Taliban started openly re-grouping, re-recruiting and re-arming in the local madrassas, without any action being taken against them by either the provincial or the federal authorities. The provincial authorities did not act because of their openly expressed sympathy for the Taliban. The federal authorities headed by Musharraf pleaded helplessness ostensibly on the ground that policing and action against suspected terrorist elements was a provincial subject over which the federal government had little control in a 'democratic set-up'.

Starting from December last year, the re-grouped Taliban began indulging in hit-and-run raids from sanctuaries in the NWFP, Balochistan and the Federally Administrated Tribal Areas (FATA) on the US and Afghan military patrols deployed in Afghan territory across the border with Pakistan. One such raid in the last week of December 2002, led to a clash between the South Waziristan Scouts, a para-military unit of Pakistan, and a US patrol, which called for an air strike on a madrassa in Pakistani territory in which the assailants had taken shelter after attacking the US troops.

This incident led to considerable anger amongst the junior-and-middle level officers of the US troops deployed in the area over the complicity of the Pakistani para-military forces with the Taliban raiders and they started demanding that they should be allowed to exercise their right of hot pursuit into Pakistani territory during their operations against the Taliban dregs based in sanctuaries in Pakistani territory. With great difficulty, the Pentagon and the State Department cooled the anger of their field officers and discouraged their talk of hot pursuit, lest such actions destabilise Musharraf.

Despite Pakistani assurances to act firmly against the Taliban raiders, such incidents continued to take place, but the numbers of the Taliban raiding parties were small and they mostly used small arms and ammunition. Moreover, they concentrated their attacks mostly on the Afghan members of the newly raised army, the police, other government workers and aid workers of non-governmental organisations and avoided direct confrontations with the US forces.

However, since August last, the frequency, magnitude, gravity and range of their attacks have increased manifold. They have often been operating in large groups numbering dozens, if not hundreds, very often move in motorised units which give them greater mobility and element of surprise and have demonstrated an ability to move far deeper into Afghan territory, even up to the outskirts of Kabul and return to their sanctuaries in Pakistan unintercepted by the Afghan and American forces.

As before, they continue to avoid direct confrontation with the American and other Western troops and have been directing their attacks mainly on Afghan government targets. Their objective is to demoralise the Afghan security forces and induce desertions in order to weaken their ability to maintain order and internal security and to convince the people that the newly raised security forces would not be able to protect them.

The seriousness of the deteriorating situation in southern and eastern Afghanistan is evident from a despatch dated 8 October 2003, sent by Ahmed Rashid, the well-known Pakistani expert on the Taliban, from Kandahar to some Western newspapers and from a media briefing in Kabul by the Bush administration's special envoy to Afghanistan, Zalmay Khalilzad, who has been designated as the new US Ambassador to Afghanistan, a nomination yet to be confirmed by the Senate.

Ahmed Rashid said in his despatch: "The Taliban army is mobilizing in Pakistan for an attack into Afghanistan before the start of winter. Up to 2,500 fighters are in Balochistan province preparing to cross the border on motorcycles and attack United States and Afghan government forces, according to Western and Afghan intelligence officials."

The Taliban have virtually taken over several suburbs of Quetta, the capital of Balochistan, and are being supported by Pakistani religious parties, the drugs mafia and al-Qaeda. There is also reportedly increasing support from the Pakistani authorities—a claim denied in Islamabad. They now plan to harry US forces in

Kandahar, where residents feel increasingly under siege, and Zabul. Since August, Taliban attacks have killed almost 400 Afghan soldiers, aid workers and civilians. Four US soldiers have also died.

"We have the American forces and the puppet regime of [President Hamid] Karzai on the run. They will collapse soon," said a Taliban mullah in Pushtunabad bazaar (of Quetta). The Taliban have bought hotels, shops and houses, forcing many frightened local residents to leave. Vehicle dealers say the Taliban have bought 900 motorcycles in the past three months in the Quetta region and another 250 in Loralai. Motorcycle guerrillas roam Afghanistan's rural areas attacking aid agency vehicles and isolated police posts. For communications, they are importing hundreds of satellite telephones from the Arab Gulf states because those bought in Pakistan are closely monitored by America's Central Intelligence Agency. Arms and ammunition are dumped inside Afghanistan. Their funding comes from the drugs trade and al-Qaeda. Osama bin Laden is still in hiding along the Pakistan-Afghanistan border.

"The Taliban are also deeply involved in the heroin trade which last year generated £717 million in Afghanistan—a sum equal to the amount spent on reconstruction aid for the country. Logistical support for the Taliban is available from the hardline mullahs of the Jamiat-ul-Ulema Islam (JUI)—a partner in the ruling coalition that governs Balochistan."

"In recent weeks President Karzai has appealed to JUI mullahs and the Pakistan army to stop the Taliban from organizing in Quetta, but that has only infuriated the JUI. 'The Afghan government and Karzai are the stooges of America and every Muslim and every Afghan knows this', said Maulana Hafiz Hussain Sharodi, Balochistan's Information Minister. 'Only the Taliban can constitute the real government in Afghanistan'."

"According to President Karzai, the headquarters for Taliban planing is the Shaldara madrassa in Quetta run by Maulana Nur Mohammed, who is a JUI member of parliament. 'We are proud that the Taliban are made and helped here,' said Maulana Abdul

Qadir, the deputy to Nur Mohammed. 'Our job is to make sure that the whole Pakistani nation supports the Taliban.' Hundreds of Pakistani Taliban are joining their Afghan brothers, although Pakistan denies that its citizens are involved."

"US officials are perturbed at the extent of Pakistani help to the Taliban and Congress has become increasingly critical. However, the White House is still reluctant to criticise President Pervez Musharraf because of America's desperate need to enlist Pakistani troops for Iraq. Yousuf Pashtun, the Governor of Kandahar province, says Pakistan has allowed the Taliban to establish six training camps in Balochistan. He accused the Pakistani authorities of 'wanting to push the Taliban into another big battle with government forces,' fearing that in the next phase 'the Taliban will start urban terrorism'." (End of citation from his despatch)

Addressing a press conference at Kabul on 7 October 2003, Zalmay Khalilzad made the following points:

- The Taliban and al-Qaeda might be planning 'larger' or 'more spectacular attacks' in Afghanistan as part of a campaign against the reconstruction process.
- "We have seen a surge in activity in recent weeks, but we also see signs that the response has been quite effective, and I think in desperation they may try, or there are indications that they may try, to do something to get a lot of attention."
- The resurgent Taliban presented a serious threat across the south and east of the country, not least on the main north-south highway between Kabul and Kandahar, a priority project supported by both President Bush and President Hamid Karzai.
- The first priority was for the government in Pakistan to stop border crossings and stop providing sanctuary to the Taliban and al-Qaeda members. "Pakistan cannot become a sanctuary for Taliban and Al-Qaeda people who want to attack Afghanistan," he said. "There has to be a decrease, and at best an end, to cross-border attacks by Taliban and Al-Qaeda people from Pakistan. I

welcome the recent actions by the Pakistani government, but we would like to see more, in fact, a lot more."

- The Taliban had exploited a power vacuum in many southern districts where the central government, because of a lack of funds and personnel, has failed to make its presence felt. A significant part of the $1.2 billion that the administration has requested for Afghanistan for the coming year will go toward expanding the central government's presence in the provinces.

The Taliban's morale and fighting capability have been bolstered by the reinforcements from the Hizb-e-Islami (HEI) headed by Gulbuddin Hekmatyar, the former favourite mujahideen of Pakistan before it created the Taliban in 1994. After the Taliban captured Kabul in September 1996, Gulbuddin and his senior associates took shelter in the Iranian territory adjoining Pakistan's Balochistan and their men were sent back to their respective villages in the Pashtun belt of Pakistan and Afghanistan to resume their normal avocation.

The Government of Iran kept Gulbuddin and his associates under strict control and saw to it that they did not indulge in any terrorist activities, but after 9/11, under US pressure, it forced them to leave the Iranian territory. They crossed over into Balochistan where they were welcomed by the ISI and the dregs of the Taliban. Gulbuddin has since managed to re-mobilise his trained men from their villages and has played an active role in helping the Taliban to re-train and re-arm its cadres.

Since August last, the Taliban officials based in Pakistan have built up a propaganda and psywar machinery to whip up hatred of the US not only amongst the people of Afghanistan and Pakistan, but also amongst the Muslims of the Gulf and West Asia. They have been using Al Jazeera and other Arab TV channels for disseminating their propaganda material prepared with the assistance of serving and retired officers of the ISI.

In a Kabul-datelined report dated 16 October 2003, *The Associated Press* (AP) gave the following details of such activities:

- "The Taliban have launched an unprecedented campaign to win money and support from Muslim militants outside Afghanistan (news—web sites) amid a resurgence by the group marked by roadside killings, ambushes and public statements boasting of their successes."
- "After remaining relatively quiet for months, a bevy of Taliban spokesmen have been turning up on Arab TV and the Pakistani media, and a handful have started making direct phone calls to the international press, including *The Associated Press.*"
- "The calls have increased in step with a bolder, bloodier insurgency that has shaken faith in the Washington-backed Afghan government's ability to assert its control, and the U.S. military's resolve at crushing the rebels."
- Omar Samad, the Afghan Foreign Ministry spokesman, said the Taliban are using the media blitz to try to get their message out to hard-liners in neighbouring Pakistan who share their strict brand of Islam. "I think it is all part of a more organized effort," he told *The Associated Press.* "They have lost much of their ability to be a real threat to the whole process of change here, but they unfortunately still have substantial support among influential groups in Pakistan with money and access to arms and manpower."
- "Most of today's Taliban fighters are not the same young men as those who fought with the militia during the U.S.-led bombing campaign in 2001, Interior Minister Ali Ahmad Jalali said recently. They are new recruits, many drawn from the poor religious madrassas of neighboring Pakistan."
- "Jalali told AP during a recent interview that several recently captured Taliban said they came to Afghanistan on the instructions of hardline Pakistani clerics, who convinced them it was every Muslim's duty to fight jihad, or holy war, against the Americans and their Afghan surrogates. One of the men said he was paid $55 in Pakistan to come and fight."
- "With Taliban leader Mullah Omar and other top figures in hiding, captured or killed, a crop of frontmen—some new,

some old names from the regime's heyday in power—has gone into high gear. Sometimes their claims sound outlandish: that the Taliban killed 10 US soldiers in fighting in September in southern Zabul province. The Americans say one special operations soldier died in a fall during a combat operation there."

- The militia also calls to take credit for recent attacks or to warn of bloody repercussions for those who collaborate with the international community. A fax sent to AP in September claimed the Taliban were behind a wave of recent killings of employees of international aid groups—often referred to as non-governmental organizations, or NGOs."
- Aid workers have been pulled from their cars and executed in southern Ghazni, Helmand and Zabul provinces in recent months. "Our government has always respected the people who are working in NGOs that really want to build Afghanistan," read the Taliban statement. "But there is another kind of NGO which only uses the name NGO but is actually working and spying for the United States. We advise Taliban all over the country to attack them and extradite them from Afghanistan."
- "A purported Taliban spokesman who calls himself Mullah Hedayatollah Akhund appeared on the Arabic television channel Al-Jazeera two weeks ago threatening resistance to the U.S.-backed government of Afghan President Hamid Karzai. Another, Mohammed Hanif, claimed responsibility for the recent assassination of an Afghan official in southern Kandahar province in a phone call to '*The News*', Pakistan's largest English-language daily."
- "The Taliban have also used the media to manage its image. One of the main Taliban spokesmen, Sayed Hamid Agha, faxed a signed letter to AP in late September to deny a widely-circulated report that Taliban fighters had threatened to disfigure Afghans who listen to music or men who shave their breads."
- "It is impossible to independently confirm the credentials of the men claiming to be Taliban spokesmen. Some professed Taliban

spokesmen are quite openly operating from Pakistan. Attiqullah Azizi, the former Taliban information minister in the eastern Afghan province of Nangarhar, has met with journalists in Pakistan. Calls and faxes from at least two purported Taliban spokesmen appear to come from the southwestern Pakistani province of Baluchistan."

- "Samad said the Taliban are using neighboring Pakistan as a center of its new PR campaign, and the presence of at least some spokesmen there is of growing concern." Almost all of them are across the border, said Samad. 'We know very well that if the authorities across the border wanted to put an end to this, they could. There is nothing to stop them from shutting them down'." (End of citation)

DESTRUCTION OF THE AL-QAEDA AND THE IIF

After disposing of the Taliban set-up, the USA turned its attention to neutralising the set-ups of the al-Qaeda and the IIF in Afghan territory. The IIF, which largely consists of the five Pakistani components-the Harkat-ul-Mujahideen (HUM), the Harkat-ul-Jihad-al-Islami (HUJI), the Lashkar-e-Toiba (LET), the Jaish-e-Mohammad (JEM) and the anti-Shia Lashkar-e-Jhangvi (LEJ)—plus some elements from the Central Asian Republics (CARs) and South-East Asia (SEA) and a large number of Arab nationals of Chechen ancestry was much easier to handle than the highly-motivated and do-or-die Arabs of the al-Qaeda.

In the IIF, the Pakistani nationals (30,000 plus) constitute the largest number followed by the Arab nationals of Chechen ancestry, who did not constitute a single, composite organisation, but used to operate in Afghanistan as members and mentors of the Taliban and the Pakistani organisations. Those from the CARs and SEA were much smaller in number and their presence in Afghanistan did not make much difference to the ground situation.

The liberation of Kabul by the Northern Alliance, with the help of American air power, and the subsequent outburst of anti-Pakistan anger in Kabul and other cities of the north led to the hasty withdrawal into Pakistan of the dregs of the Pakistani components and their Arab associates of Chechen ancestry. Similarly, the Jehadis from SEA and the CARs too withdrew into Pakistan helter-skelter. While those from SEA managed to find their way back to their countries of origin via Bangladesh where they were transported by a ship belonging to Dawood Ibrahim, the Indian mafia-cum-terrorist leader now living in Karachi with a Pakistani passport under a different name; those from the CARs, many of whom had married Pashtun women, managed to disperse themselves in the villages of the FATA.

Only the Arabs of the al-Qaeda led by bin Laden stayed put in southern and eastern Afghanistan for some weeks and put up some resistance to the Americans. After the unsuccessful operation at Tora Bora where the Americans managed to surround the al-Qaeda dregs, including bin Laden, for some days, the latter managed to escape into the FATA, from where they dispersed themselves in small groups in the main cities of Pakistan.

When the US started the second phase of the operations against the al-Qaeda and the IIF, it sought the help of the Pakistan army to seal the border with Afghanistan to prevent the dregs from escaping into Pakistan. It similarly sought the help of the Northern Alliance to prevent their escape into the CARs. While the Northern Alliance effectively sealed the escape routes to the CARs, the Pakistan army, while ostensibly sealing the escape routes into Pakistan, let the terrorists, including bin Laden, slip into the tribal belt on the Pakistan side.

It is significant that while post-9/11, there has been no major flare-up of terrorism in the CARs due to the effective sealing by the Northern Alliance, the action of the Pakistan army and the ISI in letting the terrorists escape into Pakistan and from there to other countries has led to a flare-up of terrorism in India, Indonesia, Kenya, Yemen, Morocco and Saudi Arabia.

The return of the Pakistani components of the IIF to Pakistan led to a series of terrorist attacks on Western nationals and local Christians in Karachi, Islamabad, Bhawalpur, Murree and on the Karakoram Highway. All these attacks were carried out by members of the Pakistani components of the IIF. There was no involvement of the al-Qaeda, which used the Pakistani components for having reprisal attacks on Western nationals and Christians organisations. However, some Arab nationals of Chechen ancestry and Yemeni-Balochis (of mixed Yemeni-Balochi parentage), who had joined the Pakistani organisations, were involved. For example, there was a Yemeni-Balochi involvement in the kidnapping and brutal murder of Daniel Pearl, the US journalist, in Karachi in January last year.

Initially, Musharraf took the stand that bin Laden must be dead, but after the arrest of Khalid Sheikh Mohammad, the alleged mastermind of the 9/11 terrorist strikes in the US, and his interrogation, Musharraf changed his spin and admitted that he was probably alive and hiding in the tribal belt. As an excuse for the inability of the Pakistan army to deal effectively with the sanctuaries of the al-Qaeda and the Taliban and their cross-border raids into Afghanistan, Musharraf has been claiming that all these dregs have taken shelter in inaccessible areas of the FATA where no British or Pakistani soldier has gone before.

As he does in the case of cross-border terrorism into India, he has been using the same arguments to deny Pakistani culpability in the cross-border terrorism into Afghanistan. He has been claiming that the Pakistan army is too small and ill equipped to effectively seal the border and asks if the US with its better equipment and other technical resources is not able to prevent the infiltration into Afghan territory, how can it blame the illequipped Pakistan army for not being able to stop it.

Musharraf's claims that all the dregs of the al-Qaeda and the Taliban are hiding in the inaccessible areas of the tribal belt are not correct. All the major arrests of important leaders of the al-Qaeda have so far been made from the major urban centres of Pakistan outside the tribal belt. For example, Abu Zubaidah, projected as the then No. 3 of the al-Qaeda, was arrested in March last year from the house of a functionary of the LET in Faislabad in Pakistani Punjab; Ramzi Binalshibh was arrested from a flat in Karachi belonging to Dawood Ibrahim in September last year; Khalid Sheikh Mohammad, who was also living in the same flat, managed to escape to Quetta from where he went to Rawalpindi where he was caught in the house of a women's wing leader of the Jamaat-e-Islami, which is now a member of the ruling coalition in the NWFP and Balochistan; and Waleed bin Attash, the principal suspect in the case relating to the attack on the US naval ship USS Cole at Aden in October 2000, was caught in Karachi in April last. Many minor functionaries of the al-Qaeda were also arrested in Karachi.

In an article in the prestigious *Dawn* (10 May 2003) of Karachi, Afrasiab Khattak, the highly respected Pashtun leader, has ridiculed Musharraf's contention that the dregs of the al-Qaeda were operating from inaccessible mountainous areas in the tribal belt. After pointing out the various arrests made in Karachi and other places, he wrote: "It is true that many al-Qaeda followers were arrested in the tribal agencies at a time when they were fleeing out of Afghanistan after the US military operations in Tora Bora, Zhawar and Shahikot. They entered the tribal area because that is the only available route from the afore-mentioned places for crossing over into Pakistan and moving towards safer places. But, there is no question of the numerous al-Qaeda fugitives hiding in the tribal area. There are very solid reasons for that".

"Some proclaimed offenders from the settled districts do take refuge in the tribal area, but it is done publicly and in many cases before a jirga or tribal assembly. The newcomer is introduced to everybody and the clan or family giving refuge to the person stands responsible for his conduct as long as he lives there. It is also important to know that there are no houses for rent in the area.

Everyone lives along with their kith and kin in a fortress like house that has to be defended by the residents."

"In the case of Osama bin Laden, there are additional reasons to believe that he could not have remained in the tribal area even if he had been initially there. He cannot be unaware of the news about his possible presence in the area being widely publicised. In all probability, he would have left the area to hide in the big cities that are far safer."

"It is well known to everyone that the US Army is quite active along the border with a lot of aerial surveillance and electronic monitoring. Osama cannot be such a fool as to hang out in such close vicinity of US forces, knowing fully well that they will have little hesitation in crossing the border to get him."

"In view of the past record of the present Government, it is safer to assume that it is making an effort to hide behind the so-called inaccessibility of the tribal area for the failure of its security apparatus in nabbing the most wanted fugitives. The myth of no-man's land and the wild north-west comes quite handy as a spin and as a diversion when the Government fails to muster the required political will for taking the bull of terrorism right by the horns." (End of citation)

Since April last, there have been reports from police sources in Pakistan that in view of the splintering of the al-Qaeda after Operation Tora Bora and the disruption of its command and control, bin Laden and his No. 2, Ayman Al-Zawahiri, are no longer able to coordinate the activities of the various groups taking shelter in different cities of Pakistan and elsewhere. They say that as a result, the LET is now playing the leadership and coordinator's role in the IIF and organising operations on behalf of the al-Qaeda, not only in Pakistan, but also in the Gulf and West Asia, including Iraq.

Speaking at a panel discussion on 'Terrorism in the Indian subcontinent', organized by the US-India Political Action Committee and the US-India Institute for Strategic Policy at Washington DC, on 16 July 2003, I had made the following quantitative assessment of the terrorist infrastructure in the Afghanistan-Pakistan region, which continues to threaten the world:

- *Al-Qaeda:* About 400 survivors of the 500-strong hardcore of al-Qaeda had crossed over into Pakistan from Afghanistan giving a slip to the US security forces in the beginning of last year. Of these, about 75 are estimated to have since moved over to Yemen and Saudi Arabia and 30 are estimated to have crossed over into Iran via Pakistan's Balochistan. Of the remaining, about 75 took shelter in Karachi and 220 in Punjab, the North-West Frontier Province (NWFP), Balochistan, the Federally Administered Tribal Areas (FATA), and Pakistan-Occupied Kashmir (POK). Of the 75, who took shelter in Karachi, about 50 are still holed up in various hide-outs there with the assistance of their Pakistani sympathizers and the mafia gang led by Dawood Ibrahim, who is wanted by the Indian authorities for prosecution in connection with the Mumbai (Bombay) blasts of March 1993, a precursor of mass-casualty or catastrophic terrorism. Pakistan claims to have arrested and handed over about 400 al-Qaeda members to the US. It is not clear how many of them were hard-core members, how many just sympathizers and how many Arab residents of Pakistan, who were merely suspected of being associated with al-Qaeda.
- *The Taliban:* About 5,000 survivors of the Taliban, including its Amir Mulla Mohammad Omar and other senior leaders, out of the pre-October 7, 2001, strength of 20,000 of the militia. Out of this, about 5,000 are estimated to have perished during the US air strikes and 10,000 to have dispersed to their respective villages in Afghanistan and Pakistan. The 5,000, who have taken shelter in Pakistan, have been operating against the US and allied troops in Afghanistan from their safe havens in the NWFP and Balochistan, in concert with the Hizb-e-Islami (HEI) of Gulbuddin Hekmatyar and the survivors of the Uzbek and Chechen components of the IIF.

- *The survivors of the Pakistani components of the IIF*: Before 7 October 2001, the five Pakistani components of the IIF-namely, the Harkat-ul-Mujahideen (HUM), the Harkat-ul-Jihad al Islami (HUJI), the LET, the Jaish-e-Mohammad (JEM), and the Lashkar-c-Jhangvi (LEJ)—had a total estimated strength of about 35,000 members deployed in Afghanistan to help the Taliban and al-Qaeda in their fight against the Northern Alliance (NA). Of these, about 30,000, who managed to survive the US air strikes, crossed over into Pakistan and moved over to Karachi, Pakistani Punjab and the POK.
- *The survivors of the Uzbek and Chechen components of the IIF*: About 300 have been operating from the FATA.
- *The survivors of the SEA component*: About 200, who had originally crossed over into Pakistan, have since gone back to their respective countries.
- *The HEI*: About 400 of its cadres have been operating against the Afghan and allied troops in Afghanistan from sanctuaries in the NWFP and Balochistan.

I had also given the following qualitative assessment:

- "Presuming he is alive, bin Laden is a relentlessly hunted fugitive and his powers of co-ordination, command and control have been considerably weakened and his ability to communicate with his followers dispersed in Pakistan and elsewhere has been impaired."
- "The responsibility for the co-ordination, command and control of the terrorists operating against the US and other allied troops in Afghanistan has been taken over by Gulbuddin. Though there have been very few fatal casualties suffered by the allied and Afghan forces, the persistence of the hit-and-run attacks, with some of them taking place even in Kabul, the capital, speak disturbingly of the unimpaired morale of the dregs and the local support enjoyed by them."

- "The responsibility for the co-ordination, command and control of the terrorist operations in Pakistan itself against American and other Western targets and in Jammu and Kashmir (J&K) and other parts of India against Indian targets has been taken over by the LET due to the damage suffered by the HUM and the LEJ after the arrest of many of their cadres by the Pakistani authorities following the terrorist incidents of last year in Karachi and Islamabad."
- "There has been no evidence of the involvement of any of the Arab survivors of al-Qaeda in the incidents in Afghanistan except in one near Kandahar, in which a Yemeni transporting explosives, along with some Taliban cadres, was reported to have been killed in an accidental explosion."
- "Similarly, there has been no evidence of the involvement of any of the Arab survivors of al-Qaeda in the incidents inside Pakistan itself. Those were carried out mainly by the survivors of the Pakistani components of the IIF. Some Yemeni-Balochis were involved, but they participated as members of the Pakistani components and not of al-Qaeda."
- "Of all the terrorist strikes which have taken place after 9/11 (in J&K, New Delhi, Gandhinagar and Mumbai in India, Bali in Indonesia, Mombasa in Kenya, Moscow and Chechnya in Russia, Yemen, Riyadh in Saudi Arabia and Casablanca in Morocco), the direct involvement of the Arab survivors of the al-Qaeda is suspected only in the Riyadh incident. It is assessed that the remaining strikes were carried out by the Pakistani components of bin Laden's IIF in India and by local elements operating autonomously in other countries, with the surviving al-Qaeda leadership itself playing very little leadership role."
- "The al-Qaeda survivors scattered in Pakistan have been focusing on training the fresh recruits of the Pakistani components of the IIF in their training camps in Punjab, the NWFP, Balochistan and the POK and guiding them in their operations, without actually participating in them."

- "Of the Pakistani components, the LET's infrastructure in Pakistan and Saudi Arabia has remained largely intact and it is playing an increasingly active role as the standard-bearer of the IIF. It has also been in the forefront of the moves to spread the jihad to Iraq and to intensify it there."
- "The presence of these elements in Pakistani territory and their activities from there continue to pose a serious threat not only to Indian nationals and interests, but also to the nationals and interests of the US and other members of the international community. While Pakistan's military-intelligence establishment has definitely helped the US intelligence community in some of its operations against leading al-Qaeda survivors in Pakistan, it has avoided action against the survivors of the Taliban, the Uzbek and Chechen components, the HEI and the Pakistani components."
- "In its calculation, it would need the Taliban, the HEI and the Uzbek and chechen elements for retrieving the ground lost by it in Afghanistan and the Pakistani components to keep the Indian security forces bleeding. These elements have, at the same time, an agenda extending beyond Afghanistan and India, which includes intensifying the jihad against the US not only in Iraq, but also wherever possible, including in US territory, as evidenced by the arrest of the LET cell in the US."
- "The successes of the US intelligence community in its hunt for the survivors of the al-Qaeda have thus far been limited to the non-tribal areas of Pakistan such as Punjab and Sindh. There has been hardly any success in the tribal belt and in the POK. This has been partly due to the complicity of the local administration with the survivors and partly due to the iron curtain imposed by the military-intelligence establishment in these areas to conceal the continued existence of the terrorist infrastructure there, which is meant to serve Pakistan's strategic objectives against India and the Northern Alliance in Afghanistan."

- "The main focus of the UN Security Council's resolution No. 1373 was on the need for and urgency of effective action against terrorist funding and sanctuaries. While there has been some action against funding, even if not totally effective, there has been practically no action against the sanctuaries. Presently, the Jehadi terrorist groups operating against India, the USA, Israel, the South-East Asian countries and elsewhere in the region have almost all been using sanctuaries in Pakistan, Saudi Arabia, Iran and Syria. The concerns of the international community relating to the nuclearisation of terrorism also arise from the possible dangers of weapons of mass destruction and related technology getting into the hands of Jehadi terrorists from the already declared or yet to be declared state-sponsors of international terrorism. Unless effective action is taken to end these sanctuaries and to make these states accountable for their actions, there will be no respite from terrorism in the Indian sub-continent, the US, Israel and other affected regions."

These assessments remain valid today. While there is so far no major evidence of the involvement of the al-Qaeda and the Pakistani components of the IIF in the worsening situation in Afghanistan, these elements have been gravitating towards Iraq via Iran or Saudi Arabia in order to harass the US forces there. There have been widely conflicting estimates of the number who are already involved in acts of terrorism against the US troops and their Iraqi collaborators, varying between about 200 (Pakistani police sources) and about 1,000 (Israeli sources). I am inclined to accept the lower estimate of 200. Most of those who have gone to Iraq from Pakistan are Yemeni-Balochis and Arab nationals of Chechen ancestry and have been operating in Iraq under the umbrella of the HUM and the LET. This number does not include the sacked Iraqi soldiers and Baathist Party members, who have been operating independently. New charity organisations in Pakistan such as the Al Akhtar Trust, founded by the JEM, have been funding the terrorists not only in

Pakistan and Afghanistan, but also in Iraq. The US Treasury Department has since ordered the freezing of its bank accounts on 16 October 2003.

The Jehadi terrorists have been saying that the US is at their mercy, with one leg caught in Afghanistan and the other in Iraq and that they should not miss this opportunity to teach it a lesson.

FLOW OF FUNDS TO TERRORISTS

Despite the action taken by many countries under the UN Security Council Resolution No. 1373 to freeze bank accounts, which are suspected to be used for funding terrorism, the Taliban, the al-Qaeda and the IIF have not been short of funds. The production of heroin has again emerged as an important source of funds for the terrorist organisations operating from the Afghanistan-Pakistan region. There has been a steep increase in the production of opium and heroin in southern and eastern Afghanistan. In their hunt for the dregs of the al-Qaeda and the Taliban, the US security forces have been using Afghan warlords of the pre-1992 vintage and narcotics smugglers because of their good knowledge of the topography of the area. It has been alleged that at the request of the US intelligence agencies and security forces, many narcotics barons, undergoing imprisonment in Pakistan, were got released in order to use their services; and action against opium producers and heroin smugglers was given low priority. This has contributed to the increase in the production and smuggling of heroin and in the availability of funds for the terrorist dregs.

The last one-year has also seen a tremendous increase in the remittance of funds from overseas bank accounts to accounts in Pakistan. The total remittances during this period were estimated at US $4 billion. The Pakistani authorities attributed this increase to the fact that Pakistanis living abroad have started using normal banking channels for their remittances due to fears that the use of the informal *hawala* channels as in the past might attract the suspicion of the USA's Federal Bureau of Investigation (FBI). Even if this explanation is true, it could account for the transfer of only about US $1.5 billion from overseas accounts to accounts in Pakistan.

Following suspicion that the steep increase in the remittances flowing into Pakistan might be due to the transfer of the money held overseas by the so-called Saudi charity organisations associated with terrorism to accounts in Pakistan and the use of new accounts in Pakistan by organisations based in Saudi Arabia for funding terrorism, the FBI is reported to be closely monitoring all remittances of over US $1,000 to accounts in Pakistan. The Washington correspondent of the *News*, the Pakistani daily newspaper, of 1 October 2003 reported that the Pakistani authorities have agreed to a request from the US to report to the FBI details of all such remittances.

The action taken by the Pakistani authorities against all suspected bank accounts in Pakistan continues to be an eyewash. It is alleged that in many instances the holders of the suspected accounts were alerted beforehand of the impending freezing of their accounts in order to enable them either to transfer the bulk of the balance to other accounts under different names or to withdraw them. As a result, many frozen accounts of even well known terrorists had paltry balances at the time of freezing.

On 14 June 2003, Shaukat Aziz, Pakistan's Finance Minister, placed on the table of the National Assembly a statement giving details of the accounts frozen by the authorities. In the statement figured three accounts in Peshawar banks held in the name of bin Laden and one in the name of Ayman Al-Zawahiri (name of the branch not given). Of the three accounts of bin Laden, two were joint accounts held by him along with others and one was an account only in his name. The three bin Laden accounts, according to the statement, had balances of only US $306, US $342 and US $1585 and the account of Al-Zawahiri had a balance of US $5 only.

The statement contained a remark that the account of Al-Zawahiri had remained dormant since 1993. There were no such remarks in respect of the accounts of bin Laden. Hence, they are presumed to have been active. The statement remained silent as to what were the various deposits made in the accounts and withdrawn or transferred from them before they were frozen, who were the beneficiaries, etc.

Governance and Reconstruction

The influence and authority enjoyed by President Hamid Karzai himself and the members of his Council of Ministers in the Pashtun areas of southern and eastern Afghanistan continue to be very limited. The warlords initially inducted by the US to help its forces in their hunt for the dregs of the al-Qaeda and the Taliban have become a law unto themselves, showing reluctance to obey the orders of the central government in Kabul and to share the tax revenue collected by them with the central tax authorities.

The situation has been rendered more difficult by the action of the Iranian authorities in maintaining independent channels of communication with Ismail Khan, the ruler of Herat, and often routing their economic assistance directly to him instead of through the central government in Kabul. Of late, Hamid Karzai has been trying to be more assertive and attempting to curtail the powers of the regional heads of administration and enforcing fiscal discipline on them.

The present government in Kabul is far from being accepted by the Pashtuns as adequately representing their interests. Having failed thus far in its efforts to find Pashtun political leaders, who would be acceptable to their community and at the same time be attentive to the interests of the West, the US is alleged to be once again attracted by Musharraf's idea of seeking the cooperation of what Musharraf describes as moderate Taliban. Before the Northern Alliance liberated Kabul, Musharraf had floated such an idea to prevent its entry into Kabul, but the US did not accept it at the time.

It is said that frustrated with its inability to restore normalcy, the US might now be tempted to give a try to the earlier discarded idea of Musharraf. As a result of the prevailing confusion, the progress towards the drafting of a Constitution and the holding of elections is expected to be slow and may not be completed by next year.

Having resisted thus far suggestions for giving the ISAF a role outside Kabul in order to supplement the efforts of the US-led teams to restore law and order and to promote economic development, the US has now accepted that the NATO-led ISAF could be allowed to operate outside Kabul too and an enabling resolution in this regard has also been passed by the UN Security Council. At the same time, officials associated with the NATO command and control mechanism in Kabul have clarified that the expanded role of the ISAF would be restricted to maintenance of law and order and economic and social development and would not relate to counter-insurgency or counter-terrorism in southern and eastern Afghanistan, which would continue to be handled by the US command in the area.

CONCLUSION

Since August last, the situation in Afghanistan has been deteriorating. Increasing numbers of better trained, better equipped and better led Taliban cadres operating from sanctuaries in Pakistan have stepped up their hit-and-run raids into southern and eastern Afghanistan in order to demoralise the newly-raised army and police of the Hamid Karzai government in the hope of thereby inducing large-scale desertions. Their attacks have been focused on members of the new Afghan army, police and other government departments and foreign aid workers. They have avoided direct confrontations with the US forces, lest they pursue them into Pakistani territory. As a result, while there have been nearly 400 Afghan government and civilian fatal casualties, the number of fatal American casualties has been only four. The Taliban have also set up a well-run Psychological warfare

(PSYWAR) machinery in Pakistan, which is used to add to the anti-US anger in Pakistan as well as Afghanistan. While the Hizb-e-Islami of Gulbuddin Hekmatyar has been operating jointly with the revived Taliban from Pakistani sanctuaries, the survivors of the al-Qaeda and the Pakistani components of the International Islamic Front (IIF) have been focusing on harassing the US troops in Iraq through well-motivated Jehadis infiltrated into Iraq through Iran or Saudi Arabia. The Pakistan-based Jehadi terrorists owing allegiance to bin Laden through the IIF have been calculating that if they maintain a low, but sustained level of violence in Afghanistan and Iraq without unduly provoking the Americans into massive retaliation, battle fatigue would set in and force the US government to recall its boys home before the campaign for the next year's presidential elections picks up momentum. Though the US has been saying that it is prepared for a longish stay, whatever be the cost in terms of funds and casualties in both countries, the Jehadis view this as mere bravado and have convinced themselves that the closer the elections, the weaker will be the US will to continue the fighting. The USA's continued reluctance to act against Pakistan and make it pay a prohibitive price for helping the Jehadi terrorists is coming in the way of an effective counter-terrorism strategy. Encouraged by this US reluctance, the Pervez Musharraf regime continues to keep the Jehadi terrorists alive and active in the hope of using them to retrieve the lost Pakistani influence in Afghanistan and achieve its strategic objective of forcing a change in the status quo in India's Jammu and Kashmir.

CHAPTER 9

A Profile of Islamic Resurgence in South Asia

Maj. Gen. (Retd.) Afsir Karim

Islamic fundamentalism has spread during the last two decades in Afghanistan and Pakistan. Radical Islamic groups of several hues have sprung up in both these countries which are obsessed by a belief that Islamic tenets as interpreted by them must prevail. They advocate the restoration of certain features of Islam which governed society during the lifetime of the Prophet of Islam. They consider dilution of the 'Pristine Islamic' values as a cardinal sin which cannot be pardoned. Most radical Islamic organisations justify use of force against those societies and Muslim states which do not follow their interpretation of the Shariah *and the Quran. They believe that Muslims who follow the Western secular and cultural norms are in fact non-believers who should either conform or be eliminated. The missionary zeal of Islamic fundamentalist movements and their efforts to impose rigid* Wahabi *traditions on the Muslims of the South and Central Asian regions has disturbed peace.*

The activities of Islamic fundamentalist organisations reveal that they are not really reformists, but are using the name of Islam to achieve their political objectives. They usually take up arms against those who do not cooperate. Being extremely narrow-minded and bigoted, fundamentalist groups have generated ethnic, sectarian and cultural violence in many countries in South Asia.

The policies of the countries and organisations which are promoting violence and terrorism in the name of religion must come under critical international scrutiny so that the spread of violence and terrorism is checked in the South and Central Asian regions.

THE FUNDAMENTALIST REGIME

Pakistan has been the centre of Islamic resurgence and a supporter of the Pan-Islamic movement in South Asia since its inception. 'The ideal and rationale of Pakistan State is an Islamic consensus that is expected to transcend geographic and ethnic divisions.'[1] Afghanistan, on the other hand, never deliberately mixed religion with politics in the past. To the Afghan, ethnic and tribal loyalties matter more than religious bonds.

Relations between Pakistan and Kabul were not cordial till the 1970s. They took a turn for the better only after Soviet interference began in Afghan affairs. Till the mind-1970s, Afghanistan had appeared to Pakistan as largely 'a political irritant, a petulant and resentful neighbour'.[2] In 1974, Gulbuddin Hekmatyar, and other leaders of the Islamist movement of Afghanistan, took shelter in Pakistan to escape persecution at the hands of the leftist regime. Pakistan helped these leaders to raise an army of young Afghan dissidents for covert operations against the Communist-supported regime in Afghanistan.

Hekmatyar grew to be a firebrand fundamentalist after adopting the Pan-Islamic policy of Pakistan, and around him grew an army of militant *Pushtuns.* The Soviet Union, meanwhile, had continued to promote staunch leftist groups to maintain a firm hold over Afghanistan. The seeds of a long-drawn-out conflict were thus sown in this region.

Eventually, Pakistan successfully transformed a nationalist movement against Communism into a *jihad* against 'infidel', 'godless' Communists. The warlike tribes of Afghanistan were easily motivated to wage a relentless armed struggle against the Communist-

[1]Weinbaum, Marving G. 1994 *Pakistan and Afghanistan: Resistance and Reconstruction*, p. 1. Boulder, Colorado: Westview Press.

[2]*Ibid.*, p. 13.

supported regime of their country. Later, the direct Soviet military intervention in Afghanistan gave Pakistan the opportunity to acquire the status of a front-line Islamic state, fighting the Communist onslaught. This bestowed upon Pakistan an authority to interfere in the internal affairs of Afghanistan. It was a well-calculated move to acquire a new sphere of influence and strategic space in the region after the loss of its eastern wing in 1971.

As the American and Pakistani strategic interests coincided at this point of time, Pakistan became the conduit for the supply of American arms for the Afghan resistance. It also opened the doors for generous American aid, which strengthened Pakistani military capabilities. Financial aid from Saudi Arabia steadied Pakistan's shaky economy, and gave it the confidence to take the Communist aggression next door in its stride.[3]

Saudi Arabia used this opportunity to promote *Wahabism* through the religion-based political parties of Pakistan, such as the *Jamaat-i-Islami*, which benefited greatly from Saudi Arabian patronage and grew in strength and importance. A rigid *Sunni-Wahabi* code was now being propagated with official patronage, much to the dismay of the *Shias* of Afghanistan, Pakistan and their Iranian supporters.

Some Pakistani leaders were always driven by an ambition to extend their influence beyond the Oxus into Muslim Central Asia. Pakistan manipulated the Afghan turmoil in the hope of achieving this end. It also siphoned off large quantities of sophisticated arms (and money) for launching violent political campaigns in Indian Kashmir and some parts of Central Asia. Pakistan made sure that Islamic radicalism was introduced in Afghan politics so that the training and arming of Afghan and Kashmiri terrorist groups could be carried out covertly.[4]

[3]Ibid., p. 31

[4]Behera, Ajay Darshan. 1997. 'Battle for Kabul: Interplay of Geopolitics and Cold War Logic', in *Strategic Analysis*, p. 1375. January-February. New Delhi: Institute for Defence Studies and Analyses.

Most segments of Muslims in Central Asia and Kashmir were not willing to accept rigid *Wahabi* codes, and, therefore, a programme of coercion, intimidation and terror was launched in these areas. The resentment against the imposition of a rigid *Wahabi* culture generated sectarian, ethnic and cultural violence, and sowed the seeds of internal conflicts and political upheavals in the entire region. The Inter-Services Intelligence (ISI) of Pakistan further stoked the fires by diverting sophisticated arms to terrorist groups from Afghan resistance sources. The efforts to radicalise moderate Muslim populations of India, Bangladesh and the Central Asian republics still continue. Terror is being used to overawe people to accept *Wahabi* dictates and promote Pakistani-Saudi Arab interests.

It is not entirely clear why Islamic activists needed to take recourse to terrorism to achieve their political objectives. The fact that terrorism has generally proved counter-productive in most such political confrontations is well known. To understand the motivations of Islamic militant-terrorist groups, perhaps one has to look into the doctrines and policies of two major politico-religious groups of Asia: the *Jamaat-i-Islami* (JI) of South Asia which was founded in 1941 in undivided India, and the *Ikhwan-ul-Muslemeen* ('Muslim Brotherhood') of Egypt founded in 1928 by Hassan-Al-Banna. Both the JI and the Muslim Brotherhood propagated that the divine tenets as revealed to the Prophet of Islam must form the basis of a Muslim society, and there could be no compromise with the waverers and infidels. They believe that no dilution can be accepted in the *Shariah* code of Islam as interpreted by them.[5] A brief study of some fundamentalist political groups of South Asia conducted later in this article may further clarify the mindset of these groups.

The rigid attitudes of the founders of the JI and Brotherhood leaders Abul Ala Maududi and Hassan-Al-Banna against non-Islamic societies laid the foundation of militant Islam. Sayyid Qutb, a prominent leader of the Muslim Brotherhood, advocated a bloody

[5]Esposito, John L. 1992 *The Islamic Threat: Myth or Reality?* pp. 19, 120-3. New York: Ford University Press.

revolution against the assertive secularism of Nasser in Egypt. He justified terrorism, subversion and armed *jihad* against the 'infidels'.

According to this concept, religiously motivated extremist violence was justified against those Muslims also who had strayed from the straight path, and those who refused to join the *jihad* were to be considered apostates and eliminated. This philosophy also divided the world into an abode of peace (*Dar-ul-Islam*) and an abode of war (*Dar-ul-Harb*). Extremist violence, terrorism, and confrontation against the non-Islamic world (Abode of War) was considered justified. The JI in Pakistan and the Muslim Brotherhood in Egypt continued to preach violent methods to achieve their political objectives. They were the first to create grassroots militant organisations which were armed and motivated to wage a bloody war against the 'enemies of God' and their supporters. Mosques and *madrassas* now became the focal point for spreading the message of radical Islam and the training of terrorist and subversive groups assumed an organised form.

Later, Pakistan used its religion-based parties to raise militant groups which were armed and organised for terrorism and guerrilla warfare in Bosnia, Indian Kashmir, Central Asia and Xinjiang. The support for religious war in Afghanistan and subversion and terrorism in Indian Kashmir became the two main ingredients of Pakistan's foreign policy in due course of time. Among various militant groups inducted in Kashmir, the *Hizb-ul-Mujahideen* (HM), *Harkat-ul-Ansar* (HUA) and the *Lashkar-e-Taiba* (LT) were the most motivated terrorist outfits, which drew their militant cadres from Afghan war veterans. These groups were launched in Indian Kashmir, as the subversive cadres of the JKLF were considered too soft to deal with the 'enemies of God and infidels'.[6]

Taking a leaf out of the Muslim Brotherhood philosophy of *jihad*, members of Pakistan-sponsored militant organisations were indoctrinated to believe that every Muslim was duty-bound to fight

[6]Nitesh, Sreedhar and Bhagat Nitesh. 1999. *Pakistan: A Withering State?* p. 94. Delhi: Wordsmiths.

the enemies of Islam. For this purpose, special cells were formed to organise and train small groups for subversion and terrorism. These organisations, like the *Al-Jehad* of Egypt, advocated violence in religious congregations, *Quran* study groups, welfare societies and social centres.[7]

Pakistan had trained Afghan dissidents in Miran Shah, Parachinar, Momand and Bajaur agency. *Hizb-e-Islami, Harkat-ul-Inqilab, Jamiat-e-Islami* (Afghan) were reorganised to give impetus to the *jihad* in Afghanistan. Later, these organisations and facilities were made available to the subversive and terrorist elements trained to operate in Indian Kashmir and Central Asia. A brief analysis of the Kashmir turmoil is carried out here with a view to highlight various violent phases of terrorist operations in Kashmir. The eventual failure of ruthless methods holds many lessons for those who support and advocate the use of terrorism to settle political disputes.

PAKISTAN'S COVERT OPERATIONS IN INDIAN KASHMIR

Sponsoring terrorist elements to support secessionist groups in India has been a part of Pakistan's policy for a long time. From 1985 onwards, this policy took a more concrete shape when Pakistan started training Sikh and Kashmiri terrorists together in Afghan/ Pakistani terrorist bases. Afghan instructors, initially trained by the CIA, were now employed to train these groups for operations in Indian Kashmir. The policy of using terrorism to exert pressure against perceived enemies needs to be studied in greater detail than is possible here; we will briefly examine the traumatic effects of terrorism on the common people and its inherent inability to force political changes. We are not concerned here whether the causes are morally justified or not, but with the *effects* of terrorism and violence on a peaceful society. The movement launched by the JKLF for demanding independence was hijacked by the ISI of Pakistan and

[7]Ahmed, Mumtaz. 1994. 'Islamic fundamentalism in South Asia', in Martin E. Harty and R. Scott Appleby (eds.) *Fundamentalism Observed*, p. 458. Chicago: The University of Chicago Press.

transformed into a campaign of terror. The external agencies created a reign of terror by employing force, both on the moral and physical planes. Gradually, the movement was taken over by Pakistan-sponsored radical Islamist groups, making terrorism, insurgency and ethnic cleansing its main weapons. All this, however, was presented by Pakistan's propaganda mills as a part of the indigenous Muslim uprising against Hindu India.

Terrorism was perhaps considered essential to overawe and coerce a passive and sullen Kashmiri population to rise in revolt. Brigadier Imtiaz of the ISI is credited with having masterminded a programme under which Kashmiri Muslims, Sikhs and some elements from Pakistan were trained together for subversive activities in India. By 1990, Pakistan had trained nearly 30 militant groups to operate inside Indian Kashmir. Small groups like the *Allah Tigers* and *Al-Umar* were used for terrorising the local population of the Kashmir Valley and forcing them to accept rigid *Wahabi* codes of conduct. They forcibly closed down cinema theatres, liquor shops, and attacked Christian-run schools. *Hijab* (veil) and rigid dress codes were forced on women. An obsessive desire among *Wahabis* to terrorise women can neither be easily understood nor rationalised.

A new organisation, *Ikhwan-ul-Muslimeen* (with similar aims and name as that of its Egyptian counterpart), attacked the moderate *sufi*-Islamic culture of Kashmir with extraordinary vehemence. The emphasis remained on coercion rather than persuasion, since the Kashmiri response to the call for *jihad* remained inadequate. The *Hizb-i-Islami* and its various sub-groups such as the *Nassir-ul-Islam* and *Jamaat-e-Mujahideen* were put in charge to intensify the campaign of terror. The *Janbaz Mujahideen*, a special force raised by the ISI, was given intensive training in methods of subversion and sabotage. To present this force as an indigenous product, the name of a Jammu-based organisation also called *Janbaz-Mujahideen* was adopted. The best-trained and most audacious insurgent terrorist groups were the *Hizb-i-Islami* and *Harkat-ul-Jehad*. These were infiltrated into Indian Kashmir to confront the security forces. Some of these operated in Indian Army uniforms to create an impression that the Indian Army was on the rampage against the locals.

During the most violent phase of terrorism in 1990-91, terrorist groups virtually ruled the congested urban areas of all the major towns of the Valley. They ordered *bandhs* (closure of all private and government institutions) which brought life to a standstill and created fear. The police and other key elements of the government had by now been penetrated by ISI agents, and a widening spiral of violence had engulfed the Valley. The Pakistani aim of morally and physically isolating the people from the state was largely achieved. Mass discontent and alienation forced the government to take the offensive and commit excesses against the people.

This phase took a tremendous toll of Kashmiri lives, and many popular Kashmiri leaders were gunned down for not cooperating with the terrorist groups. Discontent and resentment were now generated against the terrorists.

In the initial phase, terrorism was mainly used against three targets: symbols of state authority, non-Kashmiris, and central establishments/police forces. The people were not averse to such action, as most of them considered it just and appropriate against an unresponsive and unrepresentative government in the state.

Confrontation on the streets with the armed might of the state in thickly populated areas, however, resulted in high civilian casualties and collateral damage. When cornered, the terrorists would melt away, leaving the people to face the music. These tactics were carried beyond the tolerance of the people. The proclaimed objectives and promises of the terrorists and their sponsors in Pakistan still remained distant and unfulfilled. Over a period of time, the Indian Army successfully blunted the terrorist thrust in rural and remote areas, and people in the towns became gradually disillusioned as the terrorists failed to show material results. The elected state government was no doubt paralysed for a while, but the alternative, governor's rule, during which the elected assembly remained suspended, proved much worse for the people, who now held terrorist organisations responsible for their woes.

The agitational terrorism used successfully in the initial stages lost support as the frequent calls for *bandhs* and *hartals* (strikes) brought normal life to a standstill causing immense suffering to the common man. Closing down of schools and colleges disrupted education, and *hartals* caused great hardship to the people. The supporters of terrorism in the first phase, the local press, religious leaders, lawyers and doctors, who make public opinion, soon started evading the dictates of terrorist groups. The *Wahabi* campaign against *sufism* also became extremely unpopular as the terrorists destroyed various *Sufi* shrines dear to the people. The last straw was the indiscriminate massacre of Kashmiri Hindus by fanatical mercenary groups. The futility of mindless violence in Kashmir slowly became manifest. The people of Kashmir gradually realised that terrorism could neither bring freedom to them, nor improve their economic conditions. It was a classic example of the failure of terrorism a tool of revolution or of political reconstruction.

It must be mentioned here that, by and large, the people of the Kashmir Valley continue to be unhappy with the dispensation of the Abdullah government which came to power in 1996 through an electoral process. They are, however, ready to accept even a non-performing government, but not the reign of terror unleashed by the terrorists in the past. The latter can no longer seek shelter or creature comforts in Kashmiri homes.

On balance, it can be said that the sponsored terrorist movement in Indian Kashmir failed because it lost popular support and due to the excesses committed by the terrorists against the people of Kashmir. The terrorists failed to provide any concrete or constructive political alternative. They only wreaked vengeance on all those who refused to cooperate with them. Despite 10 years of bloody confrontation, the Pakistan-sponsored surrogate forces failed to:

- wrest away any area through armed or political action in Kashmir;
- provide relief to the people in any way (they only increased their problems and disrupted normal life); or

- transform the moderate *Sufi* culture of Kashmir into a fundamentalist ethos.

It should, however, be noted that the insurgency in Kashmir has only *subsided*, and is not yet *dead*. The next state of sponsored low-intensity conflict may be both anti-people and anti-government and extremely violent. It can cause immense destruction of life and property and bring India and Pakistan to the brink of war. Pakistan has, of course, repeatedly denied its role in supporting or sponsoring terrorism in Kashmir. The Western powers, particularly the USA, have turned a blind eye to the destructive role of Pakistan-sponsored terrorism in Indian Kashmir. If a solution to the Kashmir problem is to be found, Pakistan-sponsored terrorism must be stopped first. If peaceful conditions prevail in the Kashmir Valley and adjoining areas once again, a solution may emerge. Terrorism can only lead to increased tensions, loss of Kashmiri lives, and disruption of peace. It is quite evident that terrorism and militancy can offer no satisfactory solution to the Kashmiri problem. To understand the futility of encouraging and sponsoring terrorism, the events of Kashmir must be examined dispassionately by Pakistani leaders. It is time that Pakistan, in its own interests, stopped the violent movement in Indian Kashmir.

FUNDAMENTALIST ISLAMIC MOVEMENTS

The *Jamaat-i-Islami* (JI) of Pakistan along with its affiliated wings and the *Tablighi-Jamaat* (TJ) are the two most well-organised Islamic movements of South Asia. Both have ambitious programmes of Islamic revival, but follow divergent paths in pursuit of their objectives. The JI aims at establishing an Islamic state in Pakistan. Mumtaz Ahmad writes:

> Jamaat-i-Islami's main emphasis is on the resacralisation of political life and the establishment of an Islamic State with the *Quran* and *Sunna* (the way of the Prophet) as its constitution and *Sharia* as its basic law.

The *Tablighi* movement, on the other hand, wants to inculcate Islamic values in individual Muslims; it aims at the moral and spiritual uplift of believers, with or without an Islamic state. Both the movements are basically fundamentalist owing to their insistance on rigid adherence to the *Quranic* and *Shariah* laws as interpreted by them.[7]

They brook no compromise on the fundamentalist principles of Islam as enunciated in the Book and practised by the Prophet of Islam. The influence and activities of the JI and the *Tablighi* movement extend to most of the Muslim countries of the world. The *Tablighi Jamaat* carries out its reformist programmes even in America and Europe. Both the JI and TJ have a large number of adherents in India, Pakistan, Bangladesh and Afghanistan.

The JI stresses that Islam is a complete way of life, and that religion and politics cannot be separated. The Jamaat is, therefore, structured and organised for political activism. The TJ is basically a non-political reformist movement but its emphasis on strict adherence to Islamic values and religious practices does have an indirect political fallout in Muslim countries. The JI has well-organised and dedicated cadres, while the JI has a loose, floating organisation. The apolitical stance of the TJ has made it acceptable both in Muslim and non-Muslim societies, unlike the JI, which faces restrictions because of its religio-political agenda. The TJ has a vast subcontinental presence. Its appeal and ability to mobilise Muslim masses in India and Pakistan has various implications for the politics of the entire subcontinent.

JAMAAT-I-ISLAMI

In 1947, with the partition of British India, the JI had to split. Maududi moved to Lahore and established the JI in Pakistan. Maulana Lais Islahi of the undivided JI, a close associate of Maulana

[7]Ahmed, Mumtaz. 1994. 'Islamic fundamentalism in South Asia', in Martin E. Harty and R. Scott Appleby (eds.) *Fundamentalism Observed*, p. 458. Chicago: The University of Chicago Press.

Maududi, reorganised the JI in India as a separate entity. The Indian branch now concentrates on purely religious issues, such as Muslim personal law, and is organised as an apolitical body. The JI (Pak) and the JI (India) gradually drifted apart, maintaining only formal contact. The JI (Pak), the main branch, became an aggressive proponent of establishing an Islamic State of Pakistan. It insisted that an Islamic constitution be adopted in Pakistan which would declare the sovereignty of God and the *Shariah* as the law of the land.

The JI has well-disciplined cadres, through which it vociferously advocates fundamentalism. The organisation and programmes of the JI have served as a model for Muslim revivalism in many countries. Its aims and objectives have a striking similarity to those of the Muslim Brotherhood of Egypt, *Dar-ul-Islam* of Indonesia, the Islamic National Front of Sudan, the Islam Tendency Society in Tunis, the Parti Islam Se-Malaysia, and the Rafah party of Turkey. All these groups hope to establish an idealised Islamic system.[8]

The Islamists challenge the domination of the Western world and the inroads Western culture has made in Muslim societies. They consider themselves 'Soldiers of God' against Jewish-Christian domination. Islamic revivalism is meant to reawaken the Islamic spirit and warn Muslims against the evil practices of the Western world. They aim to revive the purity and glorious traditions of Islam.

Maulana Abul Ala Maududi, the founder of the JI, was one of the most articulate and staunch supporters of Islamic revivalism. The belligerent assertiveness propagated by the JI was meant to shock Muslims out of their apathy and indifference towards Islam. The JI justifies political activism. It believes that Islam, being a complete system, covers all aspects of a Muslim's life, and that politics, economics and culture cannot be separated from religion. The JI propagates the establishment of a complete Islamic system and is not ready to compromise on *Quranic* tenets or the examples set by the

[8] *Ibid.*, p. 459.

holy Prophet. Its vision is Pan-Islamic, but it recognises the importance of gaining political power within the existing system.

The politico-religious objectives and ideology of the JI, which it shares with the Muslim Brotherhood of Egypt, can be summarised as follows:[9]

- Islam constitutes an all-embracing ideology for individual and corporate life, for state and society.
- The *Quran*, God's revelation, and the example (*Sunna*) of the Prophet Muhammad are the foundations of Muslim life.
- Islamic Law (the *Sunna* and the 'path' of God) based upon the *Quran* and the Prophet's model behaviour, are the sacred blueprint for Muslim life.
- Faithfulness to the Muslim vocation, to re-establish God's sovereignty through the implementation of God's law will bring success, power and wealth to the Islamic community *(ummah)* in this life as well as eternal rewards in the next.
- The weakness and subservience of Muslim societies must be due to faithlessness of Muslims, who have strayed from God's divinely-revealed path and instead follow the secular, materialistic ideologies and values of the West or the East, capitalism or Marxism.
- The restoration of Muslim pride, power and rule (the past glory of Islamic empires and civilisations) require a return to Islam, the reimplementation of God's law and guidance for state and society.
- Science and technology must be harnessed and used within an Islamic-oriented and guided context in order to avoid the Westernisation and secularisation of Muslim society.

The *Jamaat-i-Islami* propagates vigorous action: to recreate the socio-religious system established under the direct guidance of the Prophet and his four successors (the rightly guided caliphs) and the establishment of the Islamic way (*al deen*) so as to achieve God's

[9]Esposito, *op. cit.*, n. 5 above, pp. 122-3.

pleasure and seek salvation in the hereafter to bring about a revolution in the political leadership of the society; reorganise socio-economic life on Islamic lines, and finally; to establish an Islamic state.[10]

Maulana Maududi and his followers reject *Sufi* Islam because of its mystic ideology which avoids competition and shuns political power. The adoption of local customs and the reverence shown to *Sufi* saints is condemned by the JI as un-Islamic.

The JI (after 1974) began a mass movement for the creation of a truly Islamic state in Pakistan. It worked resolutely to lay down the principles of an Islamic state and to prepare a new Islamic constitution for Pakistan. During the East Pakistan crisis, General Yahya Khan gave a call to the people on the Prophet's birthday to come forward and defend the ideology of Pakistan. The Jamaat, instead, organised *Shawkat-i-Islam Day* ('Glory of Islam Day'). The JI processionists also shouted slogans such as 'Socialism is *Kufr*' ('Socialism is Disbelief'). The Jamaat had earlier joined a faction of Muslims in Karachi in sponsoring a *fatwa* (religious decree) signed by more than a hundred *ulema* (religious scholars) from all schools of thought, denouncing Bhutto's socialism as *Kufr*. The JI had suspected that Z. A. Bhutto would stage a Communist-supported coup during his campaign against Ayub Khan. The Jamaat could now allow its vision of an Islamic state shattered. Therefore, the campaign against socialism and Bhutto was considered necessary.[11]

During several agitations, the workers of the Jamaat's labour and student wings clashed on the streets of Karachi, Rawalpindi and Lahore with the labour unions and the workers of Bhutto's People's Party. This confrontation transformed the *Islami-Jamaat-i-Talaba* (IJT), the students wing, from a political organisation into a militant group, ready to meet violence with violence. Militant groups of the JI collaborated with the Pakistan Army throughout the crisis in the eastern wing of Pakistan. The IJT militants were

[10]Ahmad, *op. cit.*, n. 7 above, pp. 462, 467.

[11]*Ibid.*, p. 475.

organised as a paramilitary force called *Al Badr*, which went into action against the *Mukti Bahini* in East Pakistan.

The JI and the IJT had also launched a violent campaign against the *Ahmediyas*. The JI organised a movement called *Kahtme-Nebuwwat* (belief the Muhammad was the last Prophet) with military precision and threw the law and order machinery in Pakistan totally out of gear. It also used this opportunity to arm its student wing and enlarge its membership. It was able to gain mass support for its movement for an Islamic state through dedicated grassroots workers, who were trained to use force to achieve the Jamaat's political objectives. By 1984, Jamaat-trained militant cadres had become fully involved in the Afghan war against the Soviets.

The JI gradually created efficient militant organisations which took to the streets when the necessity arose and paralysed the law and order machinery. The IJT cadres entered mosques and *madrassas* to break the monopoly of the *mullahs,* at the same time dominating student organisations and labour unions. Professional outfits and key civil and military cadres were also penetrated. It established cells in many Western countries, including the USA, to propagate militant Islam.

Maududi advocated that the Islamic tenets must be obeyed in their entirety, and a political revolution must be brought about to achieve this end. He wrote:

> The final purpose of all the blessed apostles of God was to set up the rule of God so that they could implement the entire system of life in the manner ordained by God. They were not prepared to allow the unbelievers to retain the keys of power.... That is why all prophets tried to bring about political revolutions.[12]

The political culture of the JI has remained authoritarian. Its elected president is called *Amir* who forms a *Majlis-e-Shoora* (a consultative council) elected by the members. A full-time JI worker

[12] *Ibid.*, p. 487.

is called a *rukn*. This is the hard core which fully supports and understands the ideology of Maulana Maududi. The *karkuns* are next in the hierarchy: they are the grassroots workers. They do not have the right to elect the president or his counsellors, but they are expected to spread the word of the Master. Workers of the next category are called *muttafiq*: they understand and support the ideology of the JI, but remain outside the organisation. The IJT, the militant student wing of the JI, is organised on military lines. Its members are trained to infiltrate into key organisations of the government, such as the civil services and the army. The IJT often forces closure of secular institutions and issues decrees on the dress and behaviour of women.

In Pakistan, the JI has often taken recourse to violence and used Fascist methods. Obedience to the *Amir* is considered a religious virtue, and his ideology a sacred command. The JI has a special relationship with the *Taliban*, as both share the belief in rigid and uncompromising methods of enforcing *Shariah* laws. The collaboration between the JI and the Taliban has created as climate of violence in Pakistan. They both support *Wahabism*, they are anti-*Shia*, and this has increased factional violence. Their emphasis on fundamentalism, and the desire to extend violent struggles for and wide in the name of Islam, has created political turbulence in the entire region.

The world-view of the JI is confrontational and rigid. All non-Muslims, as 'infidels', are under attack in its concept of *jihad*. Those Muslims and organisations which advocate modernism are also considered infidels; they are of the 'Party of the devil' and must be eliminated.

JAMAAT-I-ISLAMI IN KASHMIR

The JI (Kashmir) has two separate organisations, one in Pakistan-controlled Kashmir and the other in Indian Kashmir. The branch in Pakistan-controlled areas functions as an adjunct of the JI of Pakistan. The JI in Indian Kashmir has acted as a tool of subversion, creating anti-Indian feelings by promoting and encouraging fundamentalist ideas that attempt to undermine the moderate *Sufi* culture of the Kashmiri Muslims. It has been in the forefront of the political turmoil in Kashmir. Lately, however, their *Amir* declared that they were acting under fear of the gun aimed at them by the terrorists, and that they did not support violence and terrorism in principle. They believe, however, that Islamic mobilisation would ultimately result in the creation of an Islamic (Kashmiri) state. Their political thrust is currently uncertain.

JAMAAT-I-ISLAMI IN BANGLADESH

After the emergence of Bangladesh, the *Jamaat-i-Islami* was banned. It remained underground, and because of its pro-Pakistani stance it could not continue under its own name. However, it staged a remarkable comeback in many new garbs by organising local-level youth centres, mosque councils, welfare and educational associations. By the end of 1972, the Jamaat was able to set up 120 local-level units which provided a meeting place of Jamaat workers. They propagated the relinking of Bangla Muslims with Islamic states and opposed the secular constitution of Bangladesh under Sheikh Mujib-ur-Rahman. After the latter's assassination, the Jamaat formally revived its old identity. The Jamaat joined forces with Zia-ur-Rahman and succeeded in getting deleted the article in the Constitution that mentioned secularism. It was replaced with the phrase 'Absolute trust and faith in almighty Allah'.

The JI Bangladesh is now a full-fledged fundamentalist organisation which demands links with other Islamic countries to 'resist India's hegemonious designs'. The JI opposes the selling of natural gas to India and any other trade relationship. It is pro-Pakistan, and hopes to convert Bangladesh into an Islamic state that has close links with Pakistan.

THE TABLIGHI JAMAAT

The *Tablighi Jamaat* (TJ) operates throughout the subcontinent. It was founded by Maulana Mohammad Ilyas of Mewat, a district of Haryana near Delhi, in pre-Partition India. It is one of the mass religious movements launched with the aim of bringing Muslims back to the right path by persuasion and preaching. The TJ holds international meets in various parts of the world for this purpose. In 1998, it held a convention in Chicago which was attended by a large number of American Muslims. Being an apolitical organisation, the TJ has received less attention than the JI. Little is known of its methods and ultimate aims in relation to secularism and the role of Muslims in a secular society.

A *Tablighi* unit is based on 10 enlightened persons who travel and spread the Word; they instruct Muslims to follow the correct path of Islam.

The Tablighi group of 10 or *jamaat* travels far and wide. They usually assemble Muslims in village mosques. They put forward six demands, which every Muslim must accept. They preach that every Muslim should:[13]

- Recite and know the *shahadha* (that is: 'there no God but Allah and Muhammad is his Prophet'). They believe that a Muslim can develop complete faith through the *shahadha*.
- Say the *salaat* (ritual prayers five times a day) according to the prescribed rituals and format, and understand its significance.
- Do *zhikr* ceaselessly: remember God and submit to His will.
- Observe *irkam-i-muslim*: be respectful and polite to every Muslim; possess good manners and soft speech; create converts; recognise the rights of elders, neighbours, etc., to set a good example.
- Regularly travel in groups (*jamaat*) to preach Islamic values. Usually volunteers should go out for a 40-day tour called *chilla*. They preach that travel involves hardships and self-abnegation for the sake of the Almighty.

[13] *Ibid.*, p. 513.

- Understand that missionary work (*da'wa*) has to be done for the sake of Allah and not for any worldly gain.

The Tablighi movement organises hundreds of meetings in villages and small towns to enlarge the circle of true Muslims. The movement continues to grow in the entire South Asian region, countries of South East Asia, the Middle East, Europe and North America. The *Talighi Jamaat* has no fixed organisation or permanent cadres. The *Amir* and the *Majlis-e-Shoora* are elected, but they pass no formal orders to the volunteers who come forward for *da'wa*. Personal contact with individuals is considered more important than formal appeals. The TJ aims to influence ordinary Muslims, shopkeepers, teachers, doctors and other professionals.

The movement is, however, orthodox, and is aggressively anti-*Sufi*. It insists on strict adherence to the *Sunna*, but avoids political formulation of Islamic beliefs. Therefore, the individual rather than associations remains its target.

The TJ de-emphasises politics, but it has the capability to influence the political system as a good Muslim need not necessarily be apolitical. In a way the TJ is a supporting organisation of the radical and politically active *Jammat-i-Islami*. The TJ and JI, however, do not see eye to eye on most religious issues. The TJ is a reformist movement, though fundamentalist in its approach. It opposes secularism among the Muslims and does not compromise with non-Islamic practices which have taken root in Muslim societies. The TJ does not advocate violence against non-believers, and believes that the JI follows a wrong path.

CONCLUSION

Both the *Jamaat-i-Islami* and the *Tablighi* movement work on an assumption that the Muslim *ummah* must take all steps to restore true Islamic belief in the community if it has to win the ongoing battle against the 'corrupt Western culture'. They, however, follow divergent paths. Both believe that Islam can provide a more viable political alternative to the world. The militant Islamic groups of the JI consider violence against the enemies of Islam as justified and as Islam is 'God's word', it must prevail over the other religions and cultures. They treat both non-Muslims and non-practising Muslims as *kafirs* (unbelievers) and enemies of God. The TJ, on the other hand, believes that avoiding political conflicts and focusing on spiritual reawakening of Muslims will help the development of the *ummah*.

In the post-Cold War era, Islamic fundamentalism has had a great impact on the socio-political culture of the Islamic world. Militant Islam, which is an offshoot of fundamentalist beliefs, threatens the peace and tranquillity of most South Asian countries. At the political and ideological levels, Islamic fundamentalism is in a state of war against all non-Islamic states and groups. It is politico-religious movement, which replicates many of the violent methods of Marxist revolutionary movements. Guerrilla warfare and terrorism of the Islamic fundamentalist variety in South Asia have an alarming potential for disturbing peace in the entire region.

CHAPTER 10

Militant Islam and Internal Conflict in South Asia and Beyond

Ashok Kapur

The history of relations between the Muslim world and the West has been marked by conflicts and contentions. Today, the battle-field lies in the Islamic world of central, south, south-east and eastern Asia, where currently Western/Christian, Hindu/Indian, Buddhist, Chinese, Russian and Islamic influences interact. This paper examines this battlefield, using Islamic forces within Pakistan-Afghanistan and Saudi Arabia as the bases of discussion. Wahabism was the first organised manifestation of militant Islam in modern times. It indicated a shift in the ideological and military battlefield from the 'inner' Islamic world to the 'outer' Islamic world. It is a driving force in Afghanistan and it has a fallout in Pakistani politics. It has influence in Kashmir, and it may have an influence as far as the Philippines. Pakistan has emerged since the 1980s as the gateway for the organised projection of militant Islam into the region. Strategic considerations and religious affinities have enabled Pakistan to exploit the situations of internal conflict in the South Asian region. Islamic militancy is a political and military strategy which seeks to Islamicise domestic political arrangements as well as external strategic relationships.

The future relationship between militant Islam and internal conflict depends not only on the strength of militant Islam but also on the ability of regional and global forces to mobilise secular forces against militant Islamic movements.

INTRODUCTION AND CONTEXT

The contention between Islam and Christianity and between Islam and the West has been a major theme in international history. Scholarly literature clearly records this contention.[1] In the past, the encounter involved the Europeans and the Muslims. Its centre of gravity was the Mediterranean world, and its main expression was the fight between the Europeans and the Ottoman empire. Historically, this was the 'inner' Islamic world. Although Muslim cultural influence penetrated Spain, the Mediterranean Sea emerged as the buffer zone between Islam and the West. Thereafter, the struggle developed an inter-Muslim or intra-Islamic character. It became a fight between the Ottoman Turks and the Arabs, and particularly the *Wahabis*. This is the story of the 1800s. It indicated a shift in the ideological and the military battlefield from the 'inner' Islamic world to the 'outer' Islamic world. The former describes the Middle Eastern or Western Asian/Mediterranean world (where currently Western, Jewish-Israeli and Arabic influences interact; the latter describes the Islamic World of Central, South, South-east and eastern Asia (where currently Western, Hindu/Indian, Buddhist, Chinese, Russian and Islamic influences interact).[2] Historically and geographically, Afghanistan has played an important role in the 'outer Islamic world' as a gateway or the centre of gravity in the eastward spread of Islam. Peter Mansfield notes:

> Although the Arab armies conquered Sind in 712, the province was neither rich nor strategically well placed enough to serve as a base for the extention of Arab rule over the Indian sub-continent. It was not until the end of the tenth century, when Islam had been firmly established in what is now Afghanistan, that the Muslim conquest of India was begun.[3]

[1]Donohue J. L. and J. L. Esposito. 1982. *Islam in Transition*. New York: Oxford University Press. G. H. Jansen, 1979, *Militant Islam*, London: Pan Books. Peter Mansfield, 1981, *The Arabs*, New York: Penguin, 'Islam and Politics', *Third World Quarterly*, 10 (2), April 1998. I. A. Karawan, 1997, 'The Islamist Impasse', *Adelphi Paper* 314, IISS. C. K. Pullapilly (ed.), 1980, *Islam*, Notre Dame: Cross Roads Books.

[2]Mansfield, *ibid*., p. 63.

[3]*Ibid*., p. 45.

Jansen points out the importance of Afghanistan and Central Asia in the spread of Islam in another way. The Afghans fought and defeated the British in wars which had a religious and national character. Likewise, the Muslims in Central Asia thought of the Russians and their expansion as the work of *kafirs*—infidels.[4] In the context of world history and world politics, the impact of Islam now shows an element of stability (or manageable instability) in its encounter with the West, but on the other hand, there is an element of instability in its push towards the East; that is, the Islamic dimension has reached its limits in the Mediterranean world, but it continues to be a volatile and a destabilising force in the 'outer Islamic world'. The volatility is obvious in the Middle East which is geographically east of the Mediterranean, and especially in the Iran-Afghanistan-Saudi Arabian-Indian subcontinental region. It extends as well into China's Xinjiang area, and through South East Asia (Indonesia, Malaysia) upto the Philippines. That is, the encounter has moved primarily eastwards in a historical sense and perhaps in a historic way. (An exception to this remark is the situation in Algeria where Islamic forces have emerged and they have a distinctly violent and anti-Western character.)

There are three subtexts or sub-themes in the military, diplomatic and cultural history of Islam. Two of the three have contemporary significance. In managing its encounter with the Islamic world, the Western powers developed a strategy and a pattern of competitive coexistence between selected Muslim countries and Western powers. This occurred on the basis of identification of convergent strategic interests between the two sides. For example, Lawrence of Arabia mobilised the Arabs to fight and defeat the Ottoman Turks. During the Cold War, the USA developed alliances with 'moderate Muslim' countries to contain Soviet expansion. This strategy was not limited to moderate Muslim countries alone. The USA has been allied for long with Saudi Arabia, the centre of all militant *Wahabism* and an enemy of Iran. Here, the enemy of the enemy became a friend. The

[4]Jansen, *op. cit.*, note 1 above, p. 99.

USA also promoted Afghan militancy because of the common opposition to Soviet expansion into Afghanistan and the threat it posed to Western military communications in the Gulf region in the 1980s. The Western strategy of competitive coexistence and engagement of the Muslim world was also motivated by a desire to exploit the divisions between the traditional/fundamentalist versus reformer/moderniser elite within the Muslim countries. Such internal divisions helped promote internal power struggles and a preoccupation with internal politics in the 'outer' Islamic world. There is a natural affinity between the Western powers and the modernisers/reformers within the Islamic world; the West wants allies within the Islamic world, and the moderate Muslims want money and arms as well as external diplomatic and political support for their internal and external policies. Here, common strategic and economic interests create a bridge across the religious boundaries between Western Christians and Eastern Muslims; the inter-Muslim fault lines are maintained, if not enhanced as well. This subtext has historical and contemporary significance.

The second subtext was important during the Cold War and the bipolar era (1947-90), but it has now lost its salience in Islamic politics. With fresh memories of the humiliation of the colonial experience, Third World countries felt that nationalism, not Communism (or anti-Communism) was the basic and most elemental force in politics and international relations; they felt that developmental issues and North South relations ought to receive priority over military alliance politics and the East-West struggle. They shared a common fear of the great powers' domination of international and regional strategic and economic relationships. The faith in nationalism and the quest for 'third ways' to organise world politics led to assertiveness of Afro-Asian nationalism, where Muslim nationalism played an important role. These expressions of Third-World nationalism emerged in the context of the rise of many newly independent states out of the breakdown of empires and in the context of a bipolarised Cold War international system. With the end of this particular system, as the colonial memories have faded and as Third World states find it profitable to make deals with major Western powers, this subtext lacks contemporary significance.

The third subtext is very significant for our analysis: it has both historical and contemporary value. *Wahabism* was the first organised manifestation of militant Islam in modern times.[5] It is the driving force today in Afghanistan. It has influence in Chechnya.[6] It is in contention with Iranian *Shi'ite* orthodoxy, and it has a fallout in Pakistani politics as well as the politics of Kashmir, and it may have an influence as far as the Philippines.[7] In the context of the history of inter-Muslim (or intra-Muslim) ideological and military warfare, *Wahabism* plays a less powerful role. Peter Mansfield notes that:

> In 1806 the Wahhabi forces led by Amir Muhammad al-Saud occupied Mecca and had the public prayers read in his name instead of that of the Ottoman sultan. This was an Arab movement in that it was inspired by racial pride in the achievements of Muhammad and his followers in the earliest days of Islam and it was anti-Turkish in that the Wahhabis believed that the Ottoman sultans had forfeited their right to the caliphate. But its appeal was to Islamic rather than Arab solidarity. It was far removed from modern secular Arab nationalism.[8]

The distinction between the Islamic rather than the 'secular Arab nationalism' orientation in *Wahabism* is still in play today. It has

[5]*Ibid.*, p. 45.

[6]Armstrong, G. P. 1998. *Russia, The South Caucasus and The Caspian: A Handbook*, Directorate of Strategic Analysis Policy Group, Department of National Defense, Canada, August; 'The Chechen Knot', Directorate of Strategic Analysis, Department of National Defense, Canada, Research Note 98/01, February 1998.

[7]Raman, B. 'The Invisible Government and the Visible Terrorist', Institute of Topical Studies, Chennai, India, undated, pp. 17-8.

[8]Mansfield, *op. cit.*, note 1 above, p. 156. See also pp. 123, 156, 167, 219, 240 and 400 for the prominent role of *Wahabism*.

continuously opposed Communism, Zionism and Egyptian socialism.[9] It also opposes *Sufi'ism* in different parts of the world.[10]

The second major theme that has a bearing on our topic concerns the impact of Islam on Pakistani foreign and military affairs and its internal politics. While the first theme highlighted the historical and the global aspect, the second theme highlights the regional aspect with a particular emphasis on the western and the north-western side of the Indian subcontinent. The emphasis on Pakistan is justified because it has emerged, in conjunction with Saudi *Wahabism*, specially since the 1980s, as the gateway for the organised projection of militant Islam into the region: into Afghanistan, Indian Kashmir, Indian Punjab, and Chinese Xinjiang, while Afghanistan and Saudi Arabia are the gateways for the projection of militant Islam into Central Asia and segments of South East Asia. Since 1947, Islam has functioned as the crucial subtext in Pakistani external and internal affairs. The Islamic dimension has been important in Pakistani affairs in the following ways.

- In the context of the Pakistani-Indian or Muslim-Hindu cultural, diplomatic and military encounters since 1947.
- In Pakistan's quest for enlarged ideological and strategic space towards its west. Pakistan's westward orientation was expressed by a desire to develop a regional federation that involved Afghanistan, Iran and Central Asia. Prime Minister F. K. Noon spoke in 1958 of such a federation. Pakistani scholarship supported the idea of resisting Western as well as Soviet domination, because Central Asia was lost to the Soviet authorities and a 'part of the Islamic homeland is lost to the Jews'.[11] The pull of the western Islamic regions 'outside the

[9] *Ibid.*, p. 402.

[10] Jansen, *op. cit.*, n. 1 above, p. 42.

[11] Rajan, M. S. and S. Ganguly (eds.).1981. *Sisir Gupta: India and the International System*, p. 105. New Delhi: Vikas.

subcontinent, rather than to the area east of it' (although the latter was geographically and economically closer) was recognised by Western scholars.[12]

- Third, considerations of strategy as well as religious affinity have enabled Pakistan's political and military class to exploit the situations of internal conflicts in Indian Kashmir and Indian Punjab. The eastward orientation emerged, and it too was driven by a concern to enlarge Pakistan's ideological and strategic space.
- Last, despite or because of the limited electoral appeal of Pakistani Islamic parties in Pakistani politics (whether under military governments or elected ones), the Islamic constituencies have sought to enlarge their ideological and political space within Pakistan by lobbying for the adoption of an Islamic constitution, by seeking the adoption of *Shariah* law as the country's law, by the spread of *Sunni-Shia* intra-Muslim political and social violence, and by the recruitment of Islamic-motivated individuals into the Pakistani armed forces and other branches of the government machinery.

In sum, 'militant' Islam in Pakistan has an external as well as an internal orientation, and it has a westward as well as an eastward orientation.

A subtle and fundamental transformation has taken place in the role of Islam in Pakistani affairs. The shift is as follows. From the use of Islam as (*a*) a cultural reference point, (*b*) as a political option in Pakistan's internal institutional and constitutional arrangements, and (*c*) as an element in Pakistan's diplomatic strategy to build diplomatic alliances, the shifts add to the above, the use of 'militant' Islam to fan internal conflict in the neighbourhood—the latter indicates the emergence of an ideological and strategic agenda to enlarge Pakistan's external frontiers,[13] and (*d*) to enlarge the space for the Islamic

[12] *Ibid.*, p. 109.

[13] 'Frontiers' are zone(s) of competing outside influences that exist beyond a country's borders.

constituents within Pakistan and the regional neighbourhood. The shift indicates an escalation of the Islamic dimension to the military or the coercive plane. Here, Islam has emerged as a form of revolutionary violence. Among the requirements of a successful revolutionary organisation is the existence of a centrally controlled and secretive political, military and intelligence set-up which possesses the knowledge and the means to exploit the contradictions in the enemy camp.[14] Among practitioners involved in the development of revolutionary violence, the principle of territorial sovereignty is unimportant as is the Western idea of a system of sovereign states and the rule of law. Islamic militancy has the qualities of ideological and religious fanaticism. In Pakistan's case, Islamic militancy demonstrates the existence of durable connections between the following: subnational elements[15] which are politically and militarily organised and which are aligned to influential segments of the state/government; the state/government (which has an Islamicised military strategy and a military as well as paramilitary organisation in Pakistan, Afghanistan and Iran); and last, a transnational dimension exists in as much as the subnational and the statist forces in the neighbourhood outside Pakistan seek to form a mini-international Islamic society. The latter aim differs significantly from the secular base of the Western systems of states and modern international relations. In Pakistan's case, the transnationalism is twofold: the *Wahabi*-Islamic Pakistani society and government links go back to at least 1977,[16] second, the agenda of Islamic players is transnationalism as is clear by the association of the Pakistani military and intelligence agencies with the Taliban forces in the west, by their association with various militant movements and insurgencies in Indian Kashmir and Indian Punjab in the east, and by the links

[14]Fairbairn, G. 1974. *Revolutionary Guerrilla Warfare* (Harmondsworth: Penguin), outlines the methods in British India, Bolshevik Russia, Communist China, among other experiences of revolutionary change.

[15]Jansen, *op. cit.*, n. 1 above, pp. 152-4.

[16]*Ibid.*, p. 139.

with Islamic forces in Central Asia.[17] At the same time, Islamic forces have been engaged in the transformation of Pakistan into an Islamic state and society. The battlefield is, therefore, both external and internal. The growth of *Sunni-Shi'ite* violence and strife is a sign that Pakistan itself is an ideological and a military battlefield, and 'militant' Islam is not only actively involved with internal conflict in Kashmir, Punjab and Afghanistan, but engaged with internal conflict within Pakistan as well.

FROM CULTURAL AND DIPLOMATIC ISLAM TO MILITANT ISLAM: THE CASE OF PAKISTAN

The global and regional themes outlined above illustrate the emergence of three trend lines (Table 1). Fundamental shifts in the functions and impact of Islam in international, regional and domestic political theory and practice are indicated. Islamic militancy is a political and military strategy which seeks to Islamicise domestic political arrangements as well as external strategic relationships, i.e., within and between countries. The changes sought are revolutionary because they require system change and radical alteration of relationships, institutions and principles of social, political, military and economic organisations. Although it undermines the Westernised base of contemporary international relations and civil society, it nevertheless uses the territorial state as the physical base and political-diplomatic cover for Islamic militancy. The shifts may be assessed from another angle. The West-East fight during the Cold War concerned the stability of the US-Soviet military balance, but it was more than that: it involved a containment as well of Communist organisations and Communist ideology beyond the Soviet borders. It reflected an opposition to Soviet-connected revolutionary activity that sought to undermine the Westernised system of states and that sought to promote the development of a transnational society that

[17]Haynes, Jeff. 1998. *Religion in Global Politics*, ch. 8. Harlow, Essex: Longman.

was based on the principles of doctrinal war (compared to wars of fear or economic gain); that sought total war and revolutionary victory rather than inter-state compromise through negotiated political settlements; that promoted the belief that the primary loyalty of a citizen should be not to the state or the nation, but should lie with a just cause, such as Communism or Islam. So even though the Soviet-American Cold War is over, the growth of Islamic militancy points to the emergence of another kind of cold war. This cold war may be more dangerous than the one with the USSR and other Communist states, because the latter had a system of internal checks and balances within a single-party-dominated system, and the coercive machinery of the state was always subject to hierarchical party, KGB and military control and supervision. This is not the case with militant Islamic groups or political parties. The lack of institutional controls, or the existence of weak or variable controls, implies the existence of unstructured conflict in the internal as well as the external battlefields at this point in world history. Our analysis indicates that a new kind of cold war is in full swing. It emerged in the context of the first cold war, i.e., the Soviet-American (and Sino-American) Cold War(s). The Islam-centred cold war has gained a foothold in regions of conflict where vital economic and strategic interests of major and minor powers are involved. The stakes in this, the second cold war, are high because of the challenges it poses to the institution of the state, to the principle of the rule of law, to the principle that in a world of competing rights it is better to accommodate conflicting interests and competing definitions of what is right and what is wrong through a habit of compromise and compensation, rather than by warfare.

Table 1 outlines the shift from cultural-diplomatic Islam to militant Islam. There are three points of comparison, and there are three levels as well as types of shifts.

Table 1: Levels and Types of Shifts in Islam

From	*To*
	Domestic
1. Islam as a cultural reference point for Muslims in state and society.	Secure reform by peaceful means of internal political, constitutional and economic arrangements concerning national laws, government machinery and military organisation; do so by electoral means and non-violent lobbying and agitation in the country's political system.
2. Islamicisation is a peaceful political option for domestic reform.	Islam becomes a violent form of change of internal socio-economic, political and military power-sharing arrangements as well as policy development.
	External
3. Islamic ideals are a part of a country's diplomatic stance and foreign policy in the system of states.	Islamic militancy is the preferred peaceful method to expand a country's strategic, ideological and economic frontiers.

Serials 1-3 above reveal the emergence of a new framework of domestic, inter-state and transnational action and conflict in international relations today. The picture is one of fragmentation and intensified conflict, which we label as 'unstructured conflict', i.e., without well-defined, public or transparent and predictable as well as stable parameters in the decision process of the non-state actors. But an important qualification to this statement is necessary. At this point in history, the 'unstructured conflict' has the potential to become 'structured or stable conflict', with predictable parameters.

Table 2 is an attempt to identify the parameters of the dense population of players and issues as well as the patterns of alliances and enmities. Our purpose is to outline the critical mass that is inherent in the situation (with Pakistan as our case study) to illustrate the argument. We leave it to the reader to judge whether the situation outlined in Table 2 is complete and accurate, and whether it should be labeled 'unstructured' or 'structured' conflict.

Table 2: Islamic Militancy in and by the State of Pakistan

State	
Political leaders	Inter-state relations Liberation politics (Kashmir) Bureaucratic and personal politics
Pakistan Army Chief	War preparation (1947 onwards) Liberation activity (1947 onwards) Internal politics (1950s onwards); domestic targets Alliance building activity: Kashmir, Afghanistan, Central Asia Policing of 'foreign terror' groups in Pakistan
ISI (MOD) Military Intelligence and Political Division	ditto
IB (Interior Ministry)	ditto
Pakistan Foreign Office	Inter-state diplomacy Justify liberation activity

Players	Issues
Muslim League	Nature of Pakistan's constitution Promotion of Islam, with Allah as Universal Sovereign
Islamic parties and organisations[1]	ditto Intra-Muslim political and physical warfare (e.g., *Shia-Sunni*)[5] Shape/define educational system of Pakistan Organise '*madrassas*' and military training or *jihad*[5]
Ashrafs[2]	
Alafs[3]	
Mohajirs[4]	
	Society

Sources

1. Raman, B. 'The Invisible Government and the Visible Terrorist', Institute of Topical Studies, Chennai, India, no date.
2. US State Department, 'Patterns of Global Terrorism 1994', annual report. US House Republican Research Committee, Task Force on Terrorism and Unconventional Warfare, 1 February 1993.
3. Haynes, Jeff. 1998. *Religion in Global Politics*, ch. 8. London: Longman.

Notes

1. Islamic parties constitutes about 3 per cent of the electorate and do poorly in elections, but their actual influence appears to be greater than their electoral performance. There are about 85 per cent *Sunnis*, and about 15 per cent *Shias* in Pakistan.
2. *Ashrafs* are descendants of Muslim migrants into the subcontinent. *Ashrafs* were against Bangladeshis in the 1950s-1971, and against the *mohajirs.*
3. *Alafs* are descendants of Hindu converts.
4. *Mohajirs* are Muslims of Indian origin who immigrated into Pakistan.
5. About 8,000 *madrassas (Sunni)* came into being during the Zia-ul-Haq regime. They were funded allegedly by Saudi Arabia, Iraq and the CIA; the latter wanted to use motivated students to fight and bleed the Soviet forces in Afghanistan. This led to intensification of anti-*Shia* violence in Pakistan's Punjab, NWFP, Gilgit and Baltistan. Iraq responded by helping *Shia* organisations to fight *Sunni* attacks. The coalition of Pakistan government-Taliban-extremist *Sunni*-Army and *madrassas* emerged in the 1980s and it still exists in Afghanistan politics. The *Sunni-Shia* split now appears to be a permanent fracture in Pakistani and Afghan politics under the Taliban.

Table 2 indicates the emergence of linkages among four types of factors.

- The existence of a religious-ideological (Islamic) motivation to Islamicise politics and regional international relations.
- The emergence of military organisations (governmental as well as non-governmental) and the existence of budgetary support, the military capacity and the diplomatic-military strategy or a plan to change existing realities and internationally accepted norms and inter-state behaviour by coercive means.
- The existence of a fragmented geopolitical regional (external) environment that offers targets and opportunities for intervention, and that creates incentives for intervention rather than compromise. Here, the risks are deemed to be low or manageable, and even if the results are variable historically, the political rewards are deemed to be high, so the risk-reward ratio favours intervention to increase the space of the frontiers of intervening forces.
- Last, the existence of a fragmented internal environment which offers space as well as opportunities to expand the space for Islamic groups.

All four factors are necessary, but none is self-sufficient in producing a system change. The existence of internal conflict(s) in the geopolitical environment is critical because it offers the opportunity to intervene, as is the existence of internal fragmentation in a country's political structure. However, the regional geopolitical environment is the more critical factor in the following way. It is the combination of the first, second and third factors, which leads to externalisation of conflict. On the other hand, if external opportunities (in this case in Indian Punjab, Indian Kashmir, Afghanistan and Central Asia or parts of South East Asia) are reduced, then, given the durability of the first and second factors, and given the presence of the fourth factor (i.e., internal fragmentation exists) Islamic militancy will tend to turn inwards into a civil war, as in Pakistani Sind and other parts of Pakistan where intra-Muslim sectarian strife has been prominent in the 1990s. In this perspective, the regional geopolitical environment is the most important factor, because it has the potential to alter the risk-reward ratio against the Islamic forces, in comparison to the risk-reward expectations when the regional geopolitical environment is deemed to be favourable to the Islamic forces.

THE SUBCONTINENTAL TRIANGLE: THE POWERS, RELIGION AND POLITICS

The paper has examined the role of militant Islam in fanning internal conflict, but the issue is part of a wider problem and a wider international process. The wider problem is that 'Asia is out of control', as Lattimore points out in a pioneering study of Asian international relations which was published in 1949. He did not deal with the issue of militant Islam and internal conflict, but his overview and analysis is relevant to our discussion. He explains that Asia is out of control because the USA and USSR did not emerge as successors to the European empires in Asia. Asia never became truly bipolarised. There were limits to their influence in Asian affairs.[18] Lattimore highlights two aspects of the Asian situation: first, redistribution of power is (and has been) an ongoing process given the absence of bipolarised or the great powers' controls over Asians; second, the great powers were not able to emerge as successors to the European imperial powers because of the rise of nationalism in Asia. Nationalism not only limits the influence of the great powers in Asia, it also fuels the desire of newly independent countries to get a share of the available 'redistributable' power in Asia. If Lattimore is right, and the author believes he is, then the implication is that the 'redistribution' process continued in Asia even during the first cold war, despite the alleged dominance of the first cold war and the bipolar system from 1947 to 1990. Our analysis

[18]Lattimore, O. 1949. *The Situation in Asia*, pp. 36, 37 and 44. Boston: Little Brown.

is located in the belief that militant Islam is playing a regional and an international role in the perspective offered by Lattimore, and our perspective, which is outlined below.

During the first cold war, and following its end in 1990, the redistributive process has continued but it has been marked by three kinds of tensions or contradictions. There is a three-way interaction in this process involving the Western powers and China on one hand, Asian and Middle Eastern nationalism on the second, and religious/ethnic subnationalism in different parts of Asia including the Indian subcontinent. The first contradiction is between the activism of the great powers which seek to form patron-client relationships in Asia through alliance activity, aid relations and intervention in domestic politics, but on the other hand nationalistic forces have opposed the development of such dependency relationships which are deemed to be contrary to the national interest. The contradiction here is between the highly advertised Western liberal and democratic values which are projected as the moral basis of Western foreign policies, but on the other hand, Western strategic interests favour alliance activity with 'friendly' but not necessarily democratic and nationalistic forces. Consider American alliance relationships with Sygman Rhee in South Korea, the secret service organisations of Nazi Germany and imperial Japan, the Shah of Iran, F. Marcos in the Philippines, several military dictators in Pakistan, and military strongman Sukarno in Indonesia: these are examples of opportunistic alliance activity by the world's greatest democracy that is based on *interests* rather than *values.* A related contradiction is that American nationalism (or patriotism) is deemed to be just and necessary, but Asian nationalism is deemed to be narrow and dangerous to peace. (Consider that Mahatma Gandhi was refused the Nobel Prize because of his nationalism.) Yet another related contradiction is that American hegemony (global leadership, by definition) is deemed to be necessary and good, but regional hegemony (domineering behaviour, by definition) by Asian powers is considered objectionable as a danger to peace (and to US/Western leadership).

The second kind of contradiction pits nationalistic forces in China, India and other parts of Asia against the subnational religious and ethnic forces that are driven by homeland politics (independence) or by a search for power sharing (autonomy) that reflects religious and/or ethnic ideology and separateness. The contradiction here is between nationalism which seeks unity through pluralism and consensus, and on the other hand, subnationalism, which seeks unity through exclusivity in politics and which values sectarian loyalty.

The third contradiction concerns the meaning of power in Asia in the context of the redistributive process. The distribution of military and economic power is undoubtedly asymmetrical in favour of the great powers, but much of the asymmetrical power is useless in controlling fanaticism in Asia. The excess power creates overconfidence in the utility of such power, and there is a failure to deal with political problems in a psychological or a political way. Just as military problems cannot be dealt with solely by military means, political problems cannot be dealt with by purely military means. The contradiction lies in the aura of strength which asymmetrical power creates on a global or a universal scale, but if it lacks impact in a situational sense, then a contradiction exists between self-image and reality. This contradiction is very evident following the end of the first cold war and the alleged emergence of the sole superpower. Note that the US can attack Afghanistan and Sudan with cruise missiles, but it cannot eliminate the seeds of the militant philosophy of Osama bin Laden and other militant groups. The United Nations Security Council can form a broad-based international diplomatic and military front against Saddam Hussain, but it has failed to eliminate his regime despite sanctions and military action; it can harm the Iraqis but it cannot alter their attitudes and behaviour. Turkey and its allies can capture Abdullah Ochalan, the Kurdish leader, but it cannot eliminate the *idea* of Kurdistan. The USSR possessed asymmetrical power in Afghanistan in the early 1980s, but it could not win against Islamic fanaticism.

Two points need to be made about the three contradictions. First, weak countries and immature political movements (including religious ones) take advantage of the great powers' quarrels; the best they can do is to play one power against another. This results in limited success because rival powers also realise the danger of exploitation, and the major and the minor powers can also develop similar interests which can supersede their rivalries.[19] This assessment by Lattimore is quite true at the global level and even in select regional cases. For instance, the US-USSR arms control détente superseded their rivalry, as did Sino-US dètente in 1972. The Sino-American rivalry in the Korean peninsula which shaped their fight in 1950-53 has been superseded by a common interest to curb the North Korean nuclear programme. However, in the present case, common interests are not presently superseding the rivalries among the major and minor powers in the regions of conflict in Asia and the Middle East. On top of the Israel/Turkey-versus-Iraq rivalry is a US-versus-Russia rivalry for influence in the Middle East, with Russia, France and China seeking to curb US influence in Middle Eastern affairs and in the UN Security Council in relation to Iraqi issues. On top of the Turkey-versus-Iran rivalry in Central Asia is the US-versus-Russia-versus-China rivalry on the future of oil and strategy in Central Asia. On top of the Iran-versus-Saudi rivalry in the Persian Gulf is the US-versus-UK and US-versus-Russia and China rivalry for the future of the oil and arms trade and the politics of a volatile region which sits astride the communications of Central Asia, the Indian subcontinent and the Arabian Sea. On top of the *Sunni*-versus-*Shia* rivalry in Pakistan and the neighbourhood is the rivalry between Iran and Saudi Arabia, two regional powers. From these examples, it is apparent that political and religious movements in the region still enjoy the opportunities to take advantage of the quarrels among major and minor powers in Asia.

Next, the issue of militant Islam and internal conflict has a wider philosophical and strategic context: it seeks to gain power and to

[19] *Ibid.*, p. 32.

participate in the post-colonial process to redistribute power in Asia. Lattimore sheds rare insight into the role of the Western powers in supporting, possibly even engineering, the relationship between religion and politics. He points out:

> The fact that Pakistan separated from India on the issue of religious politics reveals one of the effects of British rule that nationalism has not yet been able to submerge. Encouragement of political organisation within the framework of religion had, after the First World War, become the principal British device for splitting the onslaught of a united nationalism. British official and semi-official literature persisted in referring to a supposed Hindu Congress long after the All-India Congress had made it a major policy to stress the union in nationalism of people of different religious faiths. Mohammed Ali Jinnah developed the momentum of his political career by turning this British policy to his own advantage.[20]

In other words, the future of the relationships between militant Islam and internal conflict depends not only on the strength of militant Islam, but also, and in an important way: (*a*) with the ability of regional powers to reduce the opportunities for fanning internal conflict by addressing the religious and ethnic grievances in the neighbourhood and by raising the costs of outside intervention; and (*b*) it depends as well on the policies of the major powers who are tempted to use religion to mobilise and to manipulate regional power politics as the British imperialists did in the subcontinent in the 1940s. Lattimore's analysis shows the importance of religion in Western international politics.

[20] *Ibid.*, p. 184.

Index